LEO BUSCAGLIA'S

LOVE COOKBOOK

with

BIBA CAGGIANO

LEO BUSCAGLIA'S

LOVE COOKBOOK

with
BIBA CAGGIANO

Photography by
C. STEVEN SHORT
with
SUSAN MANTLE

Styling by
BUNNY MARTIN

With a wine and food statement by
RENÉ CHAZOTTES

Published by SLACK Incorporated,
Thorofare, New Jersey

Book Design by Barbara V. Slack
Production Supervision and Direction by Linda Baker
Typesetting by Lynn Sbraga

Published by:
SLACK Incorporated
6900 Grove Road
Thorofare, NJ 08086
ISBN: 1-55642-239-3

Distributed to the trade by:
Henry Holt and Company, Inc.
115 West 18th Street
New York, NY 10011
ISBN: 0-8050-3725-X

Buscaglia, Leo F.
    Love Cookbook/by Leo F. Buscaglia with Biba Caggiano. p. cm.
    ISBN 1-55642-239-3
    1. Dinners and dining. 2. Make-ahead cookery. 3. Menus. 4. Cookery for two. I. Caggiano, Biba. II. Title
TX737.B87 1994
641.5—dc20

                                                                    94-21641
                                                                        CIP

Printed in the United States of America

10   9   8   7   6   5   4   3   2   1

TABLE OF CONTENTS

ACKNOWLEDGMENTS

One never prepares a book such as this alone. It's always a cooperative venture by many wonderful and creative individuals. They are acknowledged here with gratitude and love . . . .

Charles and Peter Slack, for their constant support;

Barbara Slack, for her creativity;

Vincent Caggiano, for his warmth and input;

Debbie Anderson, for her continual efficiency and encouragement;

René Chazottes, for sharing his expertise and love of wine;

Patty Timmens and *Juliette Jones-Moss,* for their research help;

Don Brown, chef at Biba Restaurant, Sacramento, California, for his time and talent;

Jim La Perriere, for inspiration with the "South of the Border" recipe creations;

Joe Simons, John Eichorn, and *Pam Barton,* for testing and double-checking the recipes;

Diane, Edna, and *Clancy,* for making life easier in the Biba kitchen;

Glenn Stewart, for constant, tireless assistance to Biba in managing her schedule;

Richard and Elaine Benvenuti, who allowed us to transform their handsome guest house and garden into a jumbled photo studio;

Bill Snyder of the superlative William Glen Store in Sacramento for allowing us full use of his table settings;

Darryl DuBond, Jim LeGoy, Jim Taylor, Peter Goin, Steve Davis, Ed Laine, and *Kathy Sanders* for their help in varying ways involving the photography.

INTRODUCTION

I have always been fascinated with food—the things we eat, how we prepare what we eat, and those who consume it. Food for me is more than nourishment or a necessity like sleeping and breathing. Though far from being a glutton, I tremble in anticipation of a good meal—the spicy secrets of a special preparation, the aroma of a simmering sauce, the subtleties of a fresh ripe strawberry.

I see the preparation and sharing of food as a sensuous experience—subtle, refined, artistic, appealing, voluptuous, corrupting. It involves all of our senses: sight, smell, taste, touch, and hearing—all in infinite variety.

During a perfect dinner, there is a feeling of harmony and well being among host and guests, which is difficult to describe other than to call it "love." Like love, it is a rare and wished-for thing, too delicate to fully analyze, too elusive to be verbalized.

There is agreement on three basic necessities for life: the need for food, the need for security, and the need for love. They are so intertwined that it is almost impossible to think of one without the others. When we sit at the table, there is more going on than satisfying hunger. It is this dynamic that we celebrate in our *Love Cookbook.*

When I was growing up, it seemed that opportunities for celebrating with food were far more accessible. I was raised on honest, robust, forthright Italian peasant dishes such as *polenta, risotto, minestras,* and *bagna caôda*—dishes that have recently been elevated to gourmet status. I was nurtured by the joys of the table, the warm pleasures of family dinners, and Mama and Papa moving affectionately in our small kitchen performing miracles that would soon enliven our tastebuds. I shall always remember the feeling of well being that came from being allowed to help them plan a meal, shop for it, cook it, and finally see it completed on our table. I watched with rapt interest as Mama lovingly selected each tomato that would go into her spaghetti sauce. She did this with the same loving care she used to tuck me in at night . . ."*Felice, fa la nana*." She had a God-given talent for creating gastronomical delights.

I recollect with clarity the interaction of our large family (more often than not enhanced by guests) assembling in the dining room in eager anticipation. Our togetherness made flavors more tempting; our cozy companionship precluded loneliness. It filled our souls along with our bellies.

Since we all must eat, it makes sense to use these vital occasions to the maximum. It is sad to think of those who eat simply to satisfy their hunger and who do not permit themselves to linger under the many spells offered by a good meal—the satisfaction of our hearts, our minds, and our spirits.

So all pervasive is this celebration of food that it has seeped into our language through metaphors and similes. We speak of "lips like cherries or berries." We talk of a "complexion like peaches and cream." We brag about the "apple of our eye" to whom we "bring home the bacon." We provide a "nest egg" for our "sugar" or our "honey."

Martin Elkort in his fine book, *The Secret of Food and Drink . . . History, Folklore and Fact*, says, "The search for food builds a strong appetite for words to describe them, and the words themselves become capable of stimulating the appetite by bringing forth fragrant, delicious images."

So, as the word is the poet's essential tool, food has remained the instrument of the gourmand's poetry.

My library is overflowing with books pertaining to food preparation and entertaining. There are classics written by famous gourmands that are lavishly printed and illustrated that I wouldn't dream of bringing within 100 yards of a kitchen! They are replete with recipes that call for stuffing duck necks, marinating them in Dom Perignon for at least a fortnight, and finally covering them with grated white truffles. There are cookbooks written by the rich and famous who have never seen a kitchen, let alone sweated in one. These books, mainly ghost-written, have the celebrity posed throughout the book, holding the perfect soufflé or a dish of baked Ahi in white wine, garnished with fresh mango and sauvignon grapes! There are cookbooks by professional chefs, who have managed four- and five-star restaurants in major capitals of the world. Their books suggest that if you cannot get a particular fresh ingredient or imported item and you do not have all the time in the world, you may as well hang up your apron and go out to a fine restaurant. Finally, there are those basic cookbooks usually prepared for fundraising purposes by some society or auxiliary. These exhort the merits of simple cuisine, often regional, like Aunt Tillie's favorite deep-fried chicken recipe; or Uncle Joe's Country Meatloaf. But whatever the books, I find them all engaging to own, diverting to read, and provocative to employ.

I am not a formally trained gourmet cook, though I spend many happy, contemplative hours over a burner. I am certain that this is at least partially due to the fact that Mama, also untrained, but extraordinarily creative in the kitchen, insisted that all her children learn their way around a stove, a sink, and a kitchen knife as soon as practical.

Friends will tell you that I am an enthusiastic eater. I love everything about food: the colors, shapes, aromas, tastes. I walk into a market with the same anticipation and awe as I do a museum. I never get enough until I find myself overwhelmed by the sheer bounty, and end up in a languid state of ecstasy at the checkout stand, having purchased almost everything in sight.

I do not think there is an edible item I would reject outright, though, of course, there are those I prefer over others. For example, rutabagas have never been a passion of mine; and if I never again taste some of the more exotic dishes that I was served while I ate my way around the globe, I will never miss them. But most foods bring on an ecstasy of enjoyment for me and continually stimulate my heart. And I am not alone in this. Fast foods and the much touted yearning for relief from domestic drudgery have done little to slow the advancement of the culinary arts. The joy of food just won't go away! Perhaps it is because we must eat to live, but equally significant is the insatiable human hunger for connection with self and others. More of us seem to be rediscovering the myriad of advantages inherent in the cooking, sharing, and eating of food. Cooking shows on television are extremely popular. Culinary schools everywhere are reporting packed classes. There is widespread interest in the art of cooking and entertaining. The unsung pleasures of the kitchen have come into their own. The fun of concentration and planning, the anticipation of creating that optimal experience and the resulting satisfaction are powerful rewards—rewards not frequently achieved by other labors.

So what gives me the right to coauthor a Love Cookbook? The answer is a simple one. I have been an advocate of the cause of love for most of my professional life. I was raised in a home where eating was almost a religious experience. I have been preparing and sharing food constantly for more than 60 years. During this period, I have savored the cuisine of some of the world's most illustrious cooks. And if this is not enough, I have chosen to collaborate with a sparkling chef who shares with me the same passion for life, love, and the wonder of the kitchen. She, Biba Caggiano, has written three previous best-selling cookbooks, has a popular television cooking show, and in Sacramento, California, owns and operates BIBA, one of the country's most creative and successful Italian restaurants. Who needs more fabulous credentials than these?

Biba and I share the same conviction concerning the limitless values of food experienced in love. We consider it one of the last bastions of civility, communion, and shared pleasure. We feel that sitting down at the table with lovers, friends, and families, offers another possibility for solemnizing our lives together. The table seems to be one of the only places left where we willingly rest long enough to strengthen and enliven our relationships.

We have attempted to make this lofty goal as easy, attractive, and stress free as possible. All the recipes included here are simple, delicious, and appetizing. All can be prepared at your own pace, in advance, without detracting from the taste or the look of the dish. Most importantly, no recipe in this book requires more than five to ten minutes final preparation time. This guarantees that you are free to truly enjoy your guests, both before and after the meal, rather than having to absent yourself from the fun and excitement while you frantically attempt to manipulate pots and pans in the kitchen.

So to the stimulating *littérateur gastronomique*, we bring the zestful, oft-missing and most vital ingredient for entertaining. . . *love*. Can there be a more obvious and congenial substance for pleasure, enhancement, and joy, both for ourselves and others? Is there a more persuasive seasoning? Happily, it is an element that we all possess and that is boundless. Most remarkable of all, for such a valued and exotic spice, it costs nothing! In fact, the miracle is that the more we share it, the more delicious are our rewards.

There is an old adage that states, "The way to a man's heart is through his stomach." I have no doubt that this is true, but it doesn't go far enough. The way to anybody's heart is through a thoughtfully-prepared, beautifully-executed, lovingly-presented meal. Who among us can resist such a nourishing gift, an offer so full of the promise for shared bliss? There is no medicine as powerful as joy. There is no comfort greater than being with those we love. There is no reward more satisfying than creating something with our own hands that has the power to enhance the lives of others. Love always begins with love.

THE EVOLUTION OF A COOK

"There is no spectacle on earth more appealing than that of a beautiful woman in the act of cooking dinner for someone she loves . . . ."

—Thomas Wolfe

I met Leo Buscaglia in the summer of 1982, when he came to KVIE-TV in Sacramento, to film a special for PBS. I had just completed a pilot for a half-hour cooking show that we hoped would be syndicated nationally. I was fascinated by the anecdotes of his early childhood and was immediately attracted to this charismatic man. We have kept in touch since then and have seen each other whenever possible, most often, of course, around a dinner table.

Leo's passion for good food is well known, and it was obvious to me that he was knowledgeable on the subject. A Love Cookbook had been on his mind for quite some time.

I was completely exhilarated when he asked me to collaborate with him on this project! Here we are now, with the finished product. While many of you know Leo Buscaglia because of his many best-selling books, his popular lectures, and his national television presentations, very few know me, Biba Caggiano.

I was born and raised in Bologna, Italy, a paradise for the gourmand. In 1960, I married and moved to the United States to follow my American-born husband, Vincent.

I have always loved food and am an avid eater with a well-educated palate, which has been enhanced by the succulent cuisine of my Italian region. And, as with Leo, I was literally raised in the kitchen. My mother and my grandmother were excellent cooks. This is no surprise, since most women in Bologna are notable cooks. Food there, as in most of Italy, is an integral part of everyone's life.

As a young bride living in New York City, I made an effort to recreate the everyday meals that my mother used to make. I knew how a Bolognese meat sauce was supposed to taste, as well as how much nutmeg the filling of the tortellini should have. I knew what cuts of meat I needed to produce a wonderful "bollito misto," how many hours a good broth was supposed to simmer, and how the broth was supposed to taste after the long simmering. Though this was fun, at that time in my life I was more interested in experiencing life fully outside the kitchen.

In 1969, we moved to Sacramento, a pleasant, laid-back city, without the hustle and bustle of New York. It was a great place to raise children, but, at that time, it didn't have many restaurants—especially Italian restaurants. The few that did exist served food that was virtually unrecognizable to me! It became apparent that if I wanted the wonderful food of my region, I had to cook it myself. I cooked elaborate meals for my growing family. I did a lot of entertaining. Our dinner parties were always successful, and I frequently found myself jotting down recipes for my dinner guests.

But my cooking "career" actually began because of a derogatory comment from a friend. He said he hated Italian food because he was unable to digest heavy doses of garlic, and he didn't like tomato sauces. I realized, sadly, that many Americans had the same notion. Because of the limited availability of diverse Italian delicacies, they had absolutely no idea about the richness and subtleties of one of the world's greatest cuisines. I decided to do something about it.

My first cooking class was held in my kitchen with five friends in the fall of 1977. The class was a great success in spite of my nervousness and the fact that the pupils got a bit carried away with the wine. The day after, the whole neighborhood heard about the "great cooking class." I had become a neighborhood celebrity! Six months later, in a newly opened cooking school in Sacramento, I had 20-30 students. Soon I was asked to teach up and down the West Coast. What began as a challenge to prove a point had now become a passion, almost an obsession.

I combined my many trips to Italy to visit family and friends with study tours throughout the many regions, learning all I could about the diverse culinary traditions of my land so that I could share this knowledge with my students. I developed a whole network of great Italian chefs who were eager to answer my questions. I spent time in professional kitchens sampling vast quantities of food, observing, taking notes, and peeling potatoes. One day I realized I had gone beyond the realm of "Mama's cooking," and I was moving to my own tune. And because of this, there were now a few thousand people from Portland to San Diego who regularly cooked creamy risotto, made perfect polenta, and rolled out wonderful pasta. This image gave me an overwhelming feeling of exhilaration!

After 10 years of teaching and writing three cookbooks, I was ready for another challenge. I took a big step and opened a large restaurant, BIBA. Now I was really cooking!

I was forever the teacher, showing my staff all I could about Italian food, while also taking my shift in the kitchen. I was a mother again, nurturing my customers and making sure they were thoroughly satisfied.

So, you might ask why, after all this emphasis on and dedication to Italian food, have I now changed gears and consented to work on a non-Italian cookbook? For two reasons: the joy and challenge of once again doing something new, and the exciting opportunity of working with Leo Buscaglia. Of course, even though this is not an Italian cookbook, it certainly has a strong Italian influence, because neither Leo nor I care to escape from who we are. The food in this book reflects our philosophy.

I love what good food does to people. It relaxes, soothes, nurtures, comforts, reassures, and satisfies. I've seen its magic work over the years when my husband would come home weary and exhausted after a 14-hour day with very ill patients. The moment he stepped in the house and smelled the aromas coming from the kitchen, he would say, "Wow, something smells great," and the weariness on his face would give way to a big smile. This was as great a joy for him as it was for me.

It is truer now than ever that what the world needs is more expressions of love. Breaking bread has always been seen as a form of loving, an activity at once nurturing, life enhancing, and fun.

Love is forever seeking ways of expression. Join Leo and me, through this *Love Cookbook*, in discovering yet another way of saying those ever powerful words, "I love you."

Biba

LOVING DINNERS FOR TWO

"After a perfect meal we are more susceptible to the ecstasy of love than at any other time."
—Dr. Hans Bazli

THE CARE AND FEEDING OF ROMANCE

"Here's looking at you, kid," Bogart lisped to Bergman in the movie classic "Casablanca," while gazing passionately into her beautiful eyes. Clark Gable hungrily pulled Vivian Leigh from her wagon and crushed her in his arms while Atlanta burned in "Gone With the Wind." Paul Henried lit Bette Davis' cigarette from his own, returning it sensuously to her waiting fingers in "Now Voyager." Edward, Prince of Wales, gave up a kingdom for the love of a stunning divorcee, Wallis Simpson. Romeo and Juliet defied family, friends, and society for a few brief moments of shared rapture. Dante lost his composure when he first saw Beatrice on the streets of Florence, and fainted dead away. Ah, romance! Where has it gone? What has happened to the wonderful giddiness, the anticipation, the mystery, the sheer sense of unmitigated joy of it all? What has happened to the passionate responses, the outbursts of feelings, the heroic acts? Our sensate minds have been bombarded with propaganda that romance is dead or, at best, simplistic, idealistic, and irrational nonsense. We are told that it is the unreasoning part of our personalities, the part that endlessly desires and is never satiated, maddeningly temperamental—the heart pitted against the head.

The result of society accepting this pessimistic philosophy is the irreparable loss of those fleeting but distinctive moments life offers us poor mortals. Avoiding romance may succeed in relieving us of possible pain, but it also deprives us of those rare opportunities for transcending our egos and encountering the sublime.

True, romance carried to extremes can create frustration and distress, but there is little doubt that it is primarily a highly pleasurable experience, one we should be willing to experience at any cost.

I know of no human sentiment that can surpass that of loving and being loved. In love, simple activities such as holding someone's hand, walking down the street, touching with tenderness, and sharing a meal in some intimate setting succeed in affording us that much needed escape from the mundane. We are urged on to an exciting new path: novel, thrilling, fresh.

Of all romantic experiences, a dinner at home planned around the one you love can be the greatest. It enlivens every sense. A room lit by candlelight and filled with the comforting aromas of cooking, a bottle of wine chilling on a carefully appointed table, some soft background music, and the scene is set. It's your evening—no distractions, reservations to keep, delays to endure, surly waiters or stuffy maitre d's.

"Due cose sono necessarie per sustenire la dolce vita: mangiare bene ed amare bene," so Mama told us again and again. "Two things are necessary for the maintenance of a sweet life: eat well and love well." And therein lies all you need to know.

Mama knew what she was talking about. Her sweet life reflected this philosophy for 82 years, and found its zenith in the meal shared in love, providing sustenance not only for the body, but also for the mind and the soul.

If Love is not Enough: That Ever Magical Aphrodisiac

"I shall show you a love philter without medicaments, without herbs, without witch's incantations. It is this . . . if you want to be loved, love."

—Seneca

"I'd do anything to get her to love me," a friend of mine moaned. I had the diabolical urge to inquire, "How much do you really care? Enough to eat birds' innards, cow dung, bats' wings, bull testes?" Wisely, I refrained from suggesting these highly disagreeable things as possibilities for the realization of his wish, though millions of men and women throughout history have been more than willing to resort to these extremes to attain their hearts' desires.

Since the serpent seduced Adam and Eve with an apple, endless varieties of aphrodisiacs have been offered to win over minds, hearts, and bodies. Witches and warlocks have never ceased brewing their love potions guaranteed to stimulate desire, sexual prowess, and romance. Nice people have feared speaking openly of using such devilish devices. Still, these stimulants have survived over centuries. And why not? It's understandable. We will turn to anything for relief when such a powerful need as love is frustrated. After all, we remain fallible human beings, forever in need. We will strive in any way we can to realize that promise of love.

Nothing I know is more valued than love, and nothing is more dreaded than its loss. It should not be surprising, then, that we are quick to use (or give to our lover) anything that will guarantee the love we crave. We spare no animal; we pulverize the wings of butterflies, grind the hearts of hummingbirds, mash elephants' tusks or tigers' teeth. If this appears extreme, we need only visit our local herbalist. As we peruse the merchandise, we soon discover that no tree is ignored, no plant too inaccessible, no spice too exotic, no fruit too nasty, and no cost too prohibitive if it promises success in our quest.

For example, during my travels in Southeast Asia, I was often encouraged to include durian fruit in my daily diet, in spite of the fact that I found the taste and odor so repugnant that even promises of love could not make it palatable. Durian eaters guaranteed that if I made it a part of my normal diet, I'd never be lonely again—even my dreams would be kaleidoscopes of passion. I begrudgingly did as I was bid, but the only real effects I experienced were unending attacks of gastroenteritis.

At one time or another, I have been told that bananas, peaches, avocados, and pomegranates had the magical properties that titillate passions. It was whispered to me that tomatoes were actually "love apples," that betel nuts, ginseng, kava, and passion fruit all had miraculous powers. My meals have been laced with saffron, nutmeg, dill, basil, and garlic, all with a sly smile and wink of the eye, promising a change in my love life.

Though I usually enjoyed the tastes that these savories produced, I have to admit that they were about as effective as I made up my mind for them to be. It was always intriguing to read about how useful these same agents were in aiding the infamous Madame Du Barry or the scandalous Marquis de Sade. The famous Dr. Hallick assured us for decades that his elixir was "the only sure and reliable agent for the permanent cure of impotence, sterility, and nervous and sexual disability in every form." But when it came down to reality, I found it better to rely upon the advice of the philosopher, Seneca, who suggested that if it was love I was after, I should ignore philters and medicaments and just trust in love. Still, a wise person covers all bases, neglecting none, just to be safe.

As an example, for years oysters were considered the definitive, dynamic aphrodisiac, then they suddenly fell into disrepute and were relegated to the status of a barroom joke. But oysters have had the last laugh. Modern science has revived the oyster to its original illustrious status with the discovery that it is very high in zinc, a mineral of primary importance to a healthy sex life. A three ounce serving of oysters has about four times the recommended daily allowance of zinc, which suggests all sorts of wild possibilities! If it happens that oysters are not among your favorite foods, you need not grieve. There are rich sources of zinc to be found in an abundance of foods such as liver, sunflower seeds, cheese, oats, and nuts.

As we cook our way through this book, we will overlook no food. We will freely use herbs, spices, fruits, and vegetables, not only for their unique zestful and savory properties, but also for any possible hidden enhancements they may have.

Add to this an imaginative table set for love, some fanciful and tasty combinations of easily prepared food, a wonderful wine, a whisper of music, and *voila!* the assured and consummate aphrodisiac. All bases are covered.

LOVING DINNERS FOR TWO

Starters

Leek, Spinach, and Potato Soup

Artichoke Soup

Roasted Red Bell Pepper and Asparagus Soup

Asparagus, Smoked Ham, and Parmigiano Salad

Four Cheese Salad with Roasted Walnuts

Fennel, Cucumber and Green Olive Salad

Papaya, Smoked Ham, and Figs

Mixed Wild Mushroom and Parmigiano Salad

Oysters on the Half Shell with Herb Topping

Veal Carpaccio with Capers and Parmigiano

LEEK, SPINACH, AND POTATO SOUP

Since it is totally impractical to make a batch of soup for two, the recipes in this section yield 4 to 6 servings. Any leftover soup can be kept in the refrigerator for a few days, or it can be frozen for a few weeks.

1 pound leeks	6 cups chicken broth
2 tablespoons olive oil	2 medium baking potatoes, peeled and diced
2 tablespoons unsalted butter	Salt and freshly ground pepper
1 pound fresh spinach, thoroughly washed, with stems removed	$^1/_4$ cup heavy cream

1. Cut off the root ends of the leeks and remove $^1/_3$ of the green tops. Cut the leeks in half lengthwise and slice very thinly. Place leeks in a colander and rinse well under cold water.

2. Heat the oil and butter in a medium soup pot over medium heat. Add the leeks and cook, stirring, until they begin to soften, 6 to 7 minutes. Add the spinach and 2 cups of the chicken broth. Cook 1 to 2 minutes. Add the diced potato and the remaining broth. Season with salt and pepper and bring to a boil. Reduce the heat to low and simmer, uncovered, 30 to 35 minutes.

3. Put the soup through a food mill, or purée it in a food processor, then strain it through a sieve directly back into the pot. Put the soup back on medium-low heat. Stir in the cream and simmer a few minutes. Taste, adjust the seasoning, and serve.

Prepare ahead
Through step 3, several hours or a few days ahead. Cover and refrigerate.
Reheat the soup gently just before serving.

ARTICHOKE SOUP

The California Artichoke Advisory Board tells us that "baby" artichokes are the same artichokes as their bigger counterparts. They come from the same plant. Their size is determined by their placement on the plant, which is way down among the shady plant fronds. Baby (small) artichokes are available all year round, but especially plentiful in the spring months.

3 pounds baby artichokes	**1 garlic clove, minced**
Juice of 1 lemon	**2 medium baking potatoes, peeled and diced**
2 tablespoons olive oil	
1 small yellow onion, minced	**6 cups chicken broth**
2 tablespoons fresh chopped parsley	**Salt**

1. Clean artichokes as instructed on page 91 and cut them into thin wedges. Place cleaned artichokes in a bowl of cold water with the lemon juice until ready to use.

2. Heat the oil in a medium soup pot over medium heat. Add the onion and cook, stirring, until it begins to color, 4 to 5 minutes. Add the parsley and garlic and stir a few times.

3. Drain artichokes and add to the pot. Add potatoes and broth and mix well. Season with salt and bring broth to a boil. Reduce the heat to low and simmer, uncovered, 45 minutes to 1 hour. Taste, adjust the seasoning, and serve hot.

Prepare ahead
Through step 3, several hours or a few days ahead. Cover and refrigerate.
Reheat the soup gently just before serving.

TIP: In selecting baby artichokes, or for that matter, large artichokes, choose those that are firm and compact for their size. To store, sprinkle artichokes with some water and put them in plastic bags in the coldest part of the refrigerator. They will keep for about one week.

ROASTED RED BELL PEPPER AND ASPARAGUS SOUP

This light, fresh-tasting soup has a beautiful rich golden color, a medium-thick consistency and a velvety texture. It is equally delicious served warm or at room temperature.

5 medium red bell peppers

2 tablespoons unsalted butter

2 tablespoons olive oil

1 small onion, diced

1 medium leek, white part only, thoroughly washed and diced

2 garlic cloves, minced

1 small celery stalk, diced

1 pound thin asparagus, washed and diced

1 medium baking potato, peeled and diced

1 cup dry white wine

6 cups chicken broth

Salt

$^1/_4$ cup heavy cream

1. Roast the peppers by placing them over gas burners or under a hot broiler until charred all over. Place peppers in a paper or plastic bag and leave for about 10 minutes. Peel the peppers under cold running water and remove the seeds. Cut peppers into pieces and set aside.

2. Heat butter and oil in a medium soup pot over medium heat. Add the onion, leek, and garlic. Cook, stirring, until onion begins to color, 4 to 5 minutes. Add the celery, roasted pepper, asparagus, and potato. Cook 5 to 6 minutes, stirring a few times. Add the wine and cook until it is almost all reduced, 4 to 5 minutes. Add the broth, season with salt, and bring to a boil. Reduce the heat to low and simmer uncovered, 30 to 40 minutes.

3. Put the soup through a food mill or purée it in a food processor. (This should be done in a few batches.) For a smooth, velvety soup, strain it through a sieve directly back into the pot. Put the soup back over medium-low heat and stir in the cream. Simmer a few minutes longer. Taste, adjust the seasoning, and serve hot.

Prepare ahead
Through step 3, several hours or a day ahead. Cover and refrigerate.
Reheat the soup gently just before serving.

ASPARAGUS, SMOKED HAM, AND PARMIGIANO SALAD

In this salad, I use thin asparagus simply because I prefer them. Thick asparagus are meatier than the thin ones and often are more expensive. They are also delicious. So the choice is yours. If you choose thick asparagus, peel off the fibrous outer green part of the stalks before using them.

¹/₂ pound thin asparagus

2 tablespoons extra-virgin olive oil

Juice of ¹/₂ lemon

2 ounces sliced smoked ham or prosciutto, cut into small strips

1 to 2 tablespoons freshly grated Parmigiano-Reggiano

1. Wash asparagus under cold running water. Cut off about 1 inch of the tough ends, making the asparagus all the same length.

2. Bring a large skillet half filled with salted water to a boil over medium heat. Lay the asparagus in the water and cook, gently, until tender but still a bit firm and crunchy to the taste, 2 to 3 minutes. (Thick asparagus will need an additional minute or two to cook.)

3. Drain the asparagus and place on paper towels to dry. Arrange asparagus on serving plates, cover with plastic wrap and refrigerate until ready to use.

4. Just before serving, drizzle the asparagus with oil and lemon juice, place the smoked ham or prosciutto over the asparagus, leaving the tips exposed, sprinkle with the Parmigiano, and serve.

Prepare ahead
Through step 3, several hours ahead.
Complete step 4 just before serving.

TIP: Choose fresh, green, firm asparagus spears with tight buds. If possible, try to select asparagus of the same thickness so they will cook evenly.

To keep asparagus fresh for a few days, splash them with water and place in a plastic bag. Seal bag and refrigerate. Or, place asparagus standing up in a container with a few inches of water. Cover the tips of asparagus with plastic wrap and store in the refrigerator.

FOUR CHEESE SALAD WITH ROASTED WALNUTS

This lovely appetizer can also be served as a light entrée. In that case, it could be preceded by a soup.

2 ounces whole milk mozzarella, cut into 1-inch cubes

2 ounces Gorgonzola or blue cheese cut into 1-inch cubes

2 ounces Swiss cheese, cut into 1-inch cubes

2 ounces fontina or other soft Italian or French cheese, cut into 1-inch cubes

1 ounce shelled walnuts

1 red bell pepper, roasted (see page 26), peeled, seeded, and cut into thin strips

1 tablespoon chopped fresh parsley

1 to 2 tablespoons extra-virgin olive oil

Salt and freshly ground pepper

1. Combine the cheeses in a medium bowl. Cover and refrigerate until ready to use.

2. Preheat the oven to 400°F. Place the walnuts on a cookie sheet and bake until lightly golden, 4 to 5 minutes. Cool.

3. Add walnuts, red bell pepper, parsley, and olive oil to the cheese, season with salt and several twists of pepper, and toss to mix. Taste, adjust the seasoning, and serve.

Prepare ahead
Through step 2, several hours ahead.
Complete step 3 about 15 to 20 minutes before serving.

◀ Four Cheese Salad with Roasted Walnuts

FENNEL, CUCUMBER, AND GREEN OLIVE SALAD

Fennel is a squat or elongated vegetable that has long, pale green feathery tops, a crisp consistency, and a light, delicate licorice taste. Fennel has long been a favorite of Italians and dates back to the ancient Romans. Until a few years ago, fennel was seldom available in American supermarkets, and in some parts of the United States, it is still hard to find.

1 medium fennel bulb	Salt and freshly ground pepper
1 medium cucumber, peeled and cut into thin rounds	2 to 3 tablespoons extra-virgin olive oil
10 pitted green olives, quartered	Juice of 1 small lemon
1 tablespoon minced fresh chives or Italian parsley	

1. Remove the long stalks and bruised outer leaves of the fennel and slice off the root end. Wash and dry the fennel thoroughly and cut into quarters. Cut out and discard the core of the fennel. Slice fennel lengthwise into thin strips and place in a salad bowl.

2. Place cucumber, olives, and chives in the bowl with the fennel. Season with salt and pepper and dress with the oil and lemon juice. Toss lightly, taste, adjust the seasoning, and serve.

Prepare ahead
Through step 1, a few hours ahead. Keep fennel and cucumber tightly covered in separate bowls in the refrigerator.
Complete the salad, step 2, just before serving.

TIP: If you come across this wonderful unusual vegetable, select a squat, chubby one because it is meatier and crisper than elongated fennel. A good, crisp fennel should have white, shiny leaves with no brown spots, and fresh-looking, green feathery tops. If you plan to keep fennel in the refrigerator, cut off the feathery tops and keep the bulbs well sealed in a plastic bag. It will keep for 2 to 3 days.

PAPAYA, SMOKED HAM, AND FIGS

Fresh figs are very popular in Italy and other Mediterranean countries where they are usually eaten fresh. In the United States, fresh figs have yet to make a culinary impact. Too bad, because a perfectly ripe fig is a delicious treat.

The pairing of papaya and figs with smoked ham is simply wonderful. However, since papaya might not be readily available, and fresh figs are very seasonal, a ripe melon can be substituted. Other possibilities are kiwis, mangoes, and pears.

1 firm ripe papaya (about 1 pound)	**6 thin slices smoked ham or prosciutto**
4 ripe fresh figs, washed, and patted dry	**$1/2$ lemon, seeds removed and cut into wedges**

1. Cut papaya in half lengthwise and remove the seeds. Peel and slice each half into 4 wedges. Place papaya, fanned out, in the center of two serving dishes.

2. Slice figs in halves, and place between papaya slices. Arrange ham slices loosely around fruit. Cover plates with plastic wrap and refrigerate until ready to use. Serve with lemon wedges.

Prepare ahead
Through step 2, a few hours ahead.

TIP: Of the several varieties of figs, the purple and the white are the ones most commonly available in our markets. Select a fig that is soft to the touch, has a deep color and a smooth skin with a bit of stickiness to it, which comes from the sugar content in the fig.

Papayas come from Florida, Mexico, and tropical countries. However, the majority of papayas in the United States come from Hawaii and are available all year. In selecting a papaya, look for a nice, yellow color, with a firm but yielding flesh. Do not refrigerate a papaya that is not completely ripe. You can speed the ripening process by putting it in a brown paper bag. A good papaya should have a sweet, lightly floral taste.

MIXED WILD MUSHROOM AND PARMIGIANO SALAD

Years ago, it was almost impossible to find exotic or unusual ingredients unless you lived in a large city. Today there are many specialized markets that cater to the discriminating shopper. Check with the produce department of your local supermarket, or with the specialized food market in your town, for the various mushrooms suggested in this recipe. If everything else fails, make this dish with white cultivated mushrooms.

For the Dressing

3 to 4 tablespoons olive oil, preferably extra-virgin

1 to 2 tablespoons balsamic vinegar or red wine vinegar

For the Salad

5 ounces assorted mushrooms (morels, crimini, shiitake, and chanterelles)

Salt and freshly ground pepper

4 to 5 fresh basil leaves, finely shredded or minced, or 1 teaspoon minced fresh parsley

1 ounce thinly sliced Parmigiano-Reggiano

1. In a small bowl, whisk together the oil and vinegar and set aside.

2. Wipe the mushrooms clean with a damp cloth, cut them into thin slices, and place in a medium bowl.

3. Season the mushrooms with salt and just a bit of pepper and toss with the basil or parsley and the dressing. Taste and adjust the seasoning. Arrange in small mounds on serving plates, top with the sliced Parmigiano, and serve.

Prepare ahead
Through step 2, several hours ahead.
Assemble the salad, step 3, just before serving.

TIP: Parmigiano-Reggiano is the king of Italian cheeses. Its delicious subtle flavor enriches simple and complex preparations. When buying Parmigiano, look for the words "Parmigiano-Reggiano" etched on the rind of the cheese. Real Parmigiano is a bit expensive, but a little goes a long way. Buy a small chunk, grate it as needed, and keep it tightly wrapped in the refrigerator. It will stay fresh for several weeks. The grated domestic "parmesan" found in supermarkets does little to improve the taste of your dish.

◀ Mixed Wild Mushroom and Parmigiano Salad

TIP: Balsamic vinegar is an aromatic, concentrated product made from the boiled-down must of white Trebbiano grapes. This vinegar, produced in the Emilia-Romagna region, has become a most indispensable ingredient for many serious cooks in the United States.

Balsamic vinegar falls into two categories: artisan-made and commercially-made. Artisan-made balsamic takes many decades. The boiled-down must of the grapes is aged for many years in a series of barrels of different woods, moving the contents of the barrel to another of diminishing size and wood after part of the vinegar has evaporated. This process is repeated approximately every 10 years until the final vinegar has become highly concentrated with a thick, velvety, highly-aromatic quality that defines it. Sometimes, one can find a 20- or 30-year-old balsamic vinegar. If price is no object, buy it. You will be highly rewarded. Make sure, however, that the vinegar bears the Modena consortium seal and reads "*Aceto balsamico tradizionale di Modena.*"

Most balsamic vinegar available in the United States is commercially made and is a completely different product from the artisan-made balsamic. It still can be enjoyed for what it is. Even commercially-made balsamic vinegar should be from Modena or Reggio-Emilia. Some good brands are *Fini, Giuseppe Giusti,* and *Cavalli.*

OYSTERS ON THE HALF SHELL WITH HERB TOPPING

Very fresh oysters are the essence for this delicious dish. They should have a fresh, sweet aroma. Buy them from a reputable fish market. If you have a good relationship with your fishmonger, ask to have them shucked.

Fresh oysters can be kept unopened in the refrigerator for several days. Place them curve side down in a bowl, and cover with a moist kitchen towel.

For the Herb Topping

2 tablespoons chopped fresh parsley

4 to 5 large fresh basil leaves, minced

1 garlic clove, minced

1/4 cup dry unseasoned bread crumbs

1/2 tablespoon capers, rinsed, dried, and chopped

2 tablespoons olive oil

A squeeze or two of fresh lemon juice

Salt

To Complete the Dish

1 to 1 1/2 cups rock salt

8 oysters, thoroughly scrubbed under cold running water, and shucked

1 to 2 tablespoons unsalted butter, divided into 8 small pieces

Lemon wedges

1. In a small bowl, combine all the topping ingredients into a moist mixture. Season lightly with salt and mix well. Taste and adjust the seasoning.

2. Line a small pie pan with rock salt. Shuck the oysters and drain the juices. Place each oyster on a shell. Top oysters loosely with a scant teaspoon of herb mixture and place them on the salt. (The salt will hold the oysters in place so they will not slide in the pan.) Cover with plastic wrap and refrigerate until ready to use.

3. Preheat the broiler. Remove the plastic wrap and dot each oyster with a bit of butter and place under the broiler, 3 to 4 inches from the heat source. Cook until the topping is golden brown, about 1 minute. Serve immediately with lemon wedges.

Prepare ahead
Through step 2, several hours ahead.
Complete step 3 just before serving.

VEAL CARPACCIO WITH CAPERS AND PARMIGIANO

If you are squeamish about eating raw meat, dress the meat with the oil and lemon juice and let it marinate for a few hours. The acidity in the lemon will partially cook the very thin slices of meat.

5 to 6 ounces filet of veal	**2 long green onions (white part only) washed, dried, and diced**
2 to 3 tablespoons extra-virgin olive oil	**2 tablespoons capers, rinsed, and dried**
Juice of 1/2 lemon	
Salt and freshly ground pepper	**1 ounce Parmigiano-Reggiano, cut into thin slivers**

1. Freeze the meat for about 1 hour to firm it up, then cut it into very thin slices. Put the slices between 2 sheets of plastic paper and pound them lightly until they are almost transparent. (If this seems too hard for you, ask your butcher to do it.) Arrange the slices on individual serving dishes. Cover with plastic wrap and refrigerate until ready to use.

2. Just before serving, dress the veal with oil and lemon juice and season with salt and several twists of black pepper. Top with the onion, capers, and Parmigiano, and serve.

Prepare ahead
Through step 1, several hours ahead.
Complete step 2 just before serving.

LOVING DINNERS FOR TWO

Entrées

Poached Salmon with Tomato, Cucumber,
and Olive Condiment

Shellfish in Saffron Broth

Basic Fish Broth

Swordfish Baked with Fresh Tomatoes and Capers

White Fish Baked in Parchment

Pasta with Shrimp and Fresh Tomatoes
Baked in Parchment

Roasted Chicken Breast and Avocado Salad

Pan-Roasted Chicken with Onion, Pepper, and Tomato

Turkey Brochettes with Honey and Balsamic Vinegar

Roasted Filet of Veal with Capers and Lemon Sauce

Veal Stew with Shiitake Mushrooms and Glazed Peas

Oven-Baked Veal Stew with White Wine and Artichokes

Crêpes Cannelloni with Ricotta and Smoked Ham

POACHED SALMON WITH TOMATO, CUCUMBER, AND OLIVE CONDIMENT

This method of poaching fish in a hot liquid and turning the heat off under the pot will produce very tender, delicate fish. After 10 to 15 minutes, check the doneness of your fish and if necessary, let it sit in the hot broth a bit longer. If the fish fillets are thicker than 1 inch, the cooking time should be increased a bit.

Keep the ingredients of the tomato condiment in separate bowls until ready to be assembled. Since the tomatoes will release some watery juices, you might have to strain them before mixing with the other ingredients.

For the Salmon

1 medium carrot, roughly diced

1 small onion, sliced

1 celery stalk, roughly diced

1 cup dry white wine

Salt

2 salmon fillets, $3/4$ to 1-inch thick, 7 ounces each

For the Condiment

2 medium tomatoes (about $1/2$ pound), seeded and diced

$1/2$ of a small cucumber, peeled and diced

6 to 8 pitted green olives, quartered

1 teaspoon capers, rinsed

1 large shallot, diced, or $1/4$ small mild, white onion

3 or 4 sprigs of cilantro, chopped, or 1 tablespoon chopped fresh parsley

1 small garlic clove, minced (optional)

Salt and freshly ground pepper

2 to 3 tablespoons olive oil

1 tablespoon red wine vinegar

Lemon slices

Parsley or basil sprigs

1. *To poach the salmon:* Fill a medium skillet halfway with water. Add carrot, onion, celery, parsley, wine, and 1 teaspoon of salt, and bring to a boil over high heat. Reduce the heat to medium low and simmer 20 to 25 minutes. Add the salmon and immediately remove the skillet from the heat. Leave the salmon in the hot poaching liquid for 15 to 20 minutes, or until cooked through.

2. Remove salmon and pat dry with paper towels. Arrange each fillet on a serving dish, loosely cover with foil, and chill salmon in the refrigerator.

3. *Prepare the tomato condiment:* In a medium bowl, combine all the ingredients except lemon slices and parsley sprigs, and season with salt and pepper and mix well. Taste, adjust the seasoning, and refrigerate until ready to use.

4. Just before serving, arrange condiment next to the salmon, decorate with one or two lemon slices and a sprig of fresh parsley or basil, and serve.

Prepare ahead
Through step 3, several hours ahead.
Complete step 4 just before serving.

TIP: Cilantro, also called Chinese parsley or Mexican parsley, seems to have originated in the Mediterranean. Yet, curiously enough, this flavorful herb is best known for its association with Asian and Mexican cooking. Cilantro is available all year.

In buying cilantro, look for small, bright green stems. Do not wash cilantro until ready to use; store it in a glass of water in the refrigerator, or in a plastic bag. Try to use cilantro as soon as possible to fully capture its aroma.

SHELLFISH IN SAFFRON BROTH

Saffron is made from the dried stigmas of the crocus flower, a plant native to Greece. Saffron is probably the world's most expensive spice, for it takes 75,000 stigmas to produce one pound of saffron. Saffron has a deep orange color with a pungent aroma. A small pinch of saffron can go a long way. Saffron is available as stigmas or powder.

3 cups of Basic Fish Broth (next page) or canned clam juice

2 tablespoons olive oil

$^1/_2$ medium onion, finely minced

1 garlic clove, finely minced

2 medium, ripe tomatoes, seeded and diced

1 cup dry white wine

A small pinch powdered saffron

Salt

A small pinch of chili pepper flakes

4 ounces medium shrimp, peeled and deveined

4 ounces medium sea scallops, rinsed under cold running water

4 ounces small clams, thoroughly washed under cold running water

4 ounces small mussels, thoroughly scrubbed with beard removed

1 tablespoon chopped fresh parsley

Italian or French style bread, toasted in the oven, or grilled

1. If using, prepare Basic Fish Broth as instructed on page 42.

2. Heat the oil in a medium saucepan over medium heat. Add the onion and cook, stirring, until it begins to color, 5 to 6 minutes. Add garlic and diced tomatoes, stir and cook about 1 minute. Raise the heat to high and add the wine. Cook until it is reduced by half, 3 to 4 minutes.

3. Stir the saffron into the fish broth and add to the pan. Season with salt and a small pinch of the pepper flakes. Bring broth to a boil, reduce the heat to low, and simmer, uncovered, 8 to 10 minutes.

4. Add shrimp, scallops, clams, and mussels to saucepan. Simmer 3 to 4 minutes, or until shrimp and scallops are cooked through and clams and mussels are open. Discard any shells that do not open. Stir in the parsley, taste, adjust the seasoning, and serve with toasted or grilled crusty bread.

Prepare ahead
Through step 3, several hours ahead. Cover and refrigerate.
Complete step 4 just before serving.

◀ Shellfish in Saffron Broth

BASIC FISH BROTH

A good fish broth can considerably enhance the taste of fish stews and fish soups and can be prepared with a very minimal amount of fuss. I urge you to make this broth and to keep it in your freezer. "Fish frames" can be found in fish markets. You can, however, assemble your own fish frames by freezing any piece of fish, bones, or fish parts that are not usable from another recipe.

2 pounds fish frames (fish bones, heads, odd pieces, etc.), thoroughly rinsed

1 small onion, coarsely diced

1 celery stalk, coarsely diced

1 medium carrot, cut into pieces

A few sprigs of fresh parsley

1 cup dry white wine

2 quarts cold water

Salt

1. Combine all the ingredients in a large saucepan, and bring water to a gentle boil over medium heat. Reduce the heat to low. With a slotted spoon, remove the foam that comes to the surface of the water. Simmer, uncovered, 50 minutes to one hour.

2. Pour the fish broth through a fine mesh strainer into a bowl, and cool to room temperature. It can be refrigerated for a few days or frozen up to two months. *Makes about 6 cups fish broth.*

SWORDFISH BAKED WITH FRESH TOMATOES AND CAPERS

Fresh ripe tomatoes, basil, garlic, and sun-dried tomatoes give color and taste to this dish. In this preparation, the swordfish is quickly seared, topped with the tomato mixture and baked for a short time. The swordfish can also be baked without the tomato condiment. In that case, top with fresh, uncooked condiment at the moment of serving.

Capers are the unopened flower bud of nasturtium, a wild plant native to the Mediterranean. There are two kinds of capers, the small "nonpareil" and the large "capote." They are usually pickled or packed in brine. Capers are used as an appetizing flavoring ingredient in a multitude of dishes.

4 tablespoons olive oil	**1 teaspoon sun-dried tomatoes (packed in oil), diced**
2 swordfish steaks, 1-inch thick, 7 to 8 ounces each	**1 small garlic clove, minced**
Salt and freshly ground pepper	**2 long green onions, white part only, diced**
2 small ripe plum tomatoes, seeded and cut into small cubes	**A few fresh basil leaves, finely shredded, or 1 teaspoon chopped fresh parsley**
1 teaspoon capers, rinsed	

1. In an ovenproof skillet, heat 2 tablespoons of the oil over medium-high heat. Season fish lightly with salt and pepper and add to the skillet. Cook until steaks are lightly golden on both sides, 3 to 4 minutes.

2. In a small bowl combine tomatoes, capers, sun-dried tomatoes, garlic, onions, and basil, and dress with remaining olive oil. Season with salt and pepper and mix well.

3. Preheat the oven to 350°F. Spoon tomato mixture over each steak, and bake 5 to 6 minutes, or until the fish is cooked all the way through. Serve at once.

Prepare ahead
Through step 2, one-half hour or so ahead.
Bake the fish, step 3, just before serving.

WHITE FISH BAKED IN PARCHMENT

The cooking time of fish is estimated at 10 minutes per inch of thickness. Reduce or increase the cooking time according to the thickness of your fish.

The principle of cooking in parchment is to retain the flavor and nutritive elements of the food. Food cooked in parchment also requires less fat than other cooking methods and keeps the food moist.

2 sheets of parchment paper or aluminum foil, cut into 12 × 16-inch rectangles

Olive oil to brush the parchment

2 fillets (sturgeon, halibut, or seabass), cut 1-inch thick, 6 to 7 ounces each

6 medium shrimp, peeled and deveined

6 medium sea scallops

1 medium, ripe tomato, seeded and diced

6 to 8 pitted black olives, quartered

6 to 8 fresh basil leaves, minced or 1 tablespoon chopped fresh parsley

2 tablespoons olive oil, preferably extra-virgin, mixed with 1 garlic clove, finely minced

Salt and freshly ground pepper

1. Place the two sheets of parchment paper on a work surface and brush with oil. Place 1 fillet in the center of one half of each parchment sheet. Top fillets with shrimp and scallops.

2. In a small bowl, combine diced tomatoes, olives, basil or parsley, olive oil, and garlic. Season with salt and pepper. Spoon mixture over fish. Fold the other half of the parchment sheet over the fish, and tightly fold the edges of the paper to make a 1-inch border. (Paper clips can be used to hold the folded edges.)

3. Preheat the oven to 400°F. Place the parchment bundles on a baking sheet and bake 10 to 12 minutes. (At this point, the fish should be opaque all the way through.) Transfer bundles to serving plates. Unwrap or cut the parchment with a knife or scissors, and serve the fish in its own wrapping.

Prepare ahead

Through step 2, one hour ahead. Refrigerate parchment bundles.
Complete step 3 just before serving.

PASTA WITH SHRIMP AND FRESH TOMATOES BAKED IN PARCHMENT

Sun-dried tomatoes imported from Italy are commonly found on the shelves in specialized food markets. These tomatoes have an intense fragrance and a beautiful dark red color. Italian sun-dried tomatoes are preserved in extra-virgin olive oil. The "so called" sun-dried tomatoes often found in bulk in the produce section of supermarkets do not measure up to the real thing.

4 tablespoons olive oil, preferably extra-virgin

8 ounces medium prawns, shelled and deveined

2 medium, ripe tomatoes, seeded and diced

1 tablespoon sun-dried tomatoes (packed in oil)

A pinch of chili pepper flakes

1 garlic clove, minced

1 cup dry white wine

Salt

6 to 7 ounces penne or shells

1 tablespoon chopped fresh parsley, or 5 to 6 leaves fresh basil, shredded

2 sheets of parchment paper or aluminum foil, cut into 12 × 16-inch rectangles

1. In a large skillet, heat the oil over medium-high heat. When the oil is hot, add the shrimp, and cook on both sides until lightly golden, 1 to 2 minutes. With a slotted spoon transfer shrimp to a dish.

2. Add fresh tomatoes, sun-dried tomatoes, pepper flakes, and garlic to the skillet. Cook about 1 minute, stirring constantly. Add wine. Cook until wine is almost all reduced and sauce has a medium-thick consistency, 4 to 5 minutes. Return shrimp to the skillet. Season with salt and stir once or twice. Turn the heat off under the skillet.

3. Bring a large pot of water to a boil over high heat. Add 1 teaspoon of salt and the pasta. Cook, uncovered, until pasta is only half done, 4 to 5 minutes. Drain pasta and add to the sauce. Add parsley and mix well. Taste and adjust the seasoning.

4. Place the sheets of parchment paper on a work surface and brush lightly with olive oil. Divide the pasta and sauce in half, and place in the center of one half of each parchment sheet. Fold the other half of the parchment sheet over the pasta, and tightly fold the edges of the paper to make a 1-inch border. (Paper clips can be used to hold the folded edges in place.) Place parchment bundles on a baking sheet.

5. Preheat oven to 400°F. Place bundles in the oven, and bake 8 to 10 minutes. Transfer bundles to serving plates, and carefully unwrap or cut the paper with a knife or scissors. Serve in this wrapping.

Prepare ahead

Through step 4, about an hour ahead.
Bake the pasta, step 5, just before serving.

TIP: If possible, select a brand of pasta that is imported from Italy, and is made with 100 percent semolina flour (durum wheat flour) because it is a superior product.

ROASTED CHICKEN BREASTS AND AVOCADO SALAD

Coriander is the roasted and dried seeds of Coriandrum sativum, *a plant related to parsley. Coriander is used as a flavoring agent in marinades and in many Middle Eastern dishes. Dried coriander can be found in the spice section of supermarkets.*

3 tablespoons olive oil

2 chicken breasts (8 to 10 ounces each), boned and split, with skin on

Salt and freshly ground pepper

1 large ripe avocado, peeled, pitted and cubed

6 long green onions, white parts only

1 teaspoon dry coriander seeds, crushed

1/2 small garlic clove, minced

1/2 teaspoon of finely minced jalapeño pepper (optional)

2 to 3 tablespoons olive oil

Juice of 1 lemon

2 medium tomatoes, cut into round slices

1. Preheat the oven to 400°F.

2. *Prepare the chicken:* In an ovenproof skillet, heat the oil over medium-high heat. Season chicken lightly with salt and pepper and add to the skillet, skin side down. Cook until skin is golden brown, 2 to 3 minutes, then turn and brown the other side, 1 to 2 minutes. Place chicken in the oven and bake 10 to 12 minutes, or until meat is cooked all the way through. Remove from oven and cool to room temperature. Slice the chicken into 1/4-inch strips and set aside until ready to use.

3. *Prepare the salad:* In a small bowl, combine avocado, onions, coriander, garlic, and jalapeño (if using), and season with salt and several twists of pepper. Add olive oil and lemon juice and mix gently.

4. Place sliced chicken in the center of serving dishes, arrange tomatoes around chicken and top tomatoes with the avocado salad. (Drizzle some of the salad dressing over the chicken and serve.)

Prepare ahead
Through step 2, one or two hours ahead.
Complete step 4 about one half hour before serving.

PAN-ROASTED CHICKEN WITH ONION, PEPPER, AND TOMATO

3 tablespoons olive oil

2 chicken breasts, (8 to 10 ounces each), split and boned, with skin on

Salt and freshly ground pepper

1 large red bell pepper, cored, seeded, and cut into thin strips

1 medium onion, thinly sliced

1 large tomato, seeded and diced

1 garlic clove, minced

$1/2$ cup dry white wine

A handful of fresh basil leaves, finely shredded, or 1 tablespoon chopped fresh parsley

1. Heat the oil in a medium skillet over medium-high heat. Season chicken lightly with salt and pepper, then add to the skillet, skin side down. Cook until skin is golden brown, 2 to 3 minutes, then turn and brown the other side, 1 to 2 minutes. Transfer chicken to a plate.

2. Add the bell pepper, onion, and tomato to the skillet and cook, stirring, until vegetables begin to color, 5 to 6 minutes. Add the garlic, and stir once or twice. Add the wine and cook briskly until it is reduced by half, about 2 minutes.

3. Return chicken to the skillet. Reduce the heat to low and cover with the lid slightly askew. Cook 12 to 15 minutes, or until the chicken is cooked all the way through. Stir a few times during cooking. Remove chicken and set aside.

4. Stir basil into the sauce. Taste and adjust the seasoning. Spoon vegetables into the center of two serving dishes, arrange the chicken on top, and serve.

Prepare ahead
Through step 3, one or two hours ahead of time.
Reheat chicken over moderate heat and complete step 4 just before serving.

TURKEY BROCHETTES WITH HONEY AND BALSAMIC VINEGAR

4 tablespoons honey

3 tablespoons balsamic or red wine vinegar

3 tablespoons olive oil

³/₄ pound boned, skinned turkey breast, cut into 1 ¹/₂-inch cubes

1 small red onion cut into wedges

Salt and freshly ground pepper

1. In a small bowl, combine honey, vinegar, and 1 tablespoon of the oil. Mix well to blend.

2. Thread the turkey on two metal skewers alternating the turkey with the onion, and place in a shallow dish. Pour the marinade over the turkey, and season with salt and pepper. Marinate about 1 hour, turning the skewers a few times.

3. Preheat oven to 375°F. Heat the remaining oil in a large ovenproof skillet over medium-high heat. When oil is very hot, add the skewers (reserving the marinade), and cook until turkey is golden on all sides, 4 to 5 minutes. Discard the fat in the skillet, and stir in half of the marinade.

4. Bake 12 to 15 minutes, or until the turkey is cooked all the way through. Baste a few times during cooking. If necessary, add a bit more marinade.

5. Remove meat and onion from the skewers (if you are using metal skewers, be careful because they will be hot), and arrange on serving dishes. Brush or spoon the thickened pan juices over the turkey and onion and serve.

Prepare ahead
Through step 4, one half hour or so ahead.
Complete step 5 just before serving.

ROASTED FILET OF VEAL WITH CAPERS AND LEMON SAUCE

In this preparation, the veal is browned on top of the stove ahead of time and at the last moment finished cooking in the oven. The sauce for the veal is prepared quickly and is spooned over the veal slices.

3 tablespoons olive oil

1 pound whole filet of veal

Salt and freshly ground pepper

$^1/_2$ cup dry white wine

2 tablespoons lemon juice

1 tablespoon capers, rinsed

$^1/_2$ tablespoon unsalted butter

1 tablespoon chopped fresh parsley

1. Preheat the oven to 400°F.

2. Heat the oil in an ovenproof skillet over medium-high heat. Season the veal lightly with salt and pepper and add to skillet. Cook until veal is golden on all sides, 3 to 4 minutes.

3. Place veal in the oven and bake, uncovered, 10 to 12 minutes. At this point, the veal should be golden brown on the outside and pink and juicy on the inside. Place veal on a cutting board, and let it rest while you make the sauce.

4. Put skillet back over high heat and add wine, lemon juice, capers, and butter. Cook and stir until sauce begins to thicken, 1 to 2 minutes. Add parsley and stir once or twice. Slice the veal and place in serving dishes. Spoon thickened sauce over the veal and serve at once.

Prepare ahead
Through step 3, one half hour or so ahead of time.
Complete dish, step 4, just before serving.

TIP: Keep the ingredients for the sauce—wine, lemon juice, capers, and butter—lined up on a small tray near the stove to expedite the making of the sauce.

◄ Roasted Filet of Veal with Capers and Lemon Sauce

VEAL STEW WITH SHIITAKE MUSHROOMS AND GLAZED PEAS

In this preparation, the veal is cooked slowly with the onion, mushrooms, wine, and broth until it is meltingly tender. The peas are cooked separately to retain their color and texture, then are tossed with the butter, sugar, and vinegar and added to the stew at the last moment. The sweet and sour taste of the peas, and the delicious aroma and taste of the shiitake mushrooms, give this stew its character. If shiitake mushrooms are unavailable, substitute white cultivated mushrooms or 1 ounce of dried Italian porcini mushrooms. If you are using the dried porcini mushrooms, soak them in lukewarm water for 20 minutes, then rinse them well and add to the stew as instructed in the recipe.

3 tablespoons olive oil	1 cup dry white wine
1 pound veal shoulder or stewing veal, cut into 2-inch pieces	1 cup chicken broth
	Salt
$^{1}/_{3}$ cup all-purpose flour	$^{1}/_{2}$ cup shelled fresh or thawed frozen peas
$^{1}/_{2}$ medium onion, thinly sliced	
	1 tablespoon unsalted butter
4 ounces shiitake mushrooms, wiped clean and thinly sliced	1 tablespoon sugar
1 garlic clove, minced	2 to 3 tablespoons red wine vinegar

1. Heat the oil in a medium skillet over medium-high heat. Place veal in a large colander over a bowl and add the flour. Shake the colander to evenly distribute the flour on the veal. Add the veal to the skillet in moderate batches, and brown on all sides, 5 to 6 minutes. Scoop up the browned veal with a slotted spoon, draining it against the side of the skillet. Transfer to a plate.

2. Add the onion to the skillet and cook, stirring, until the onion is pale yellow, 4 to 5 minutes. Add the shiitakes and garlic and cook until the mushrooms are lightly colored, 2 to 3 minutes. Return veal to the skillet, and add the wine. Cook and stir until wine is reduced by half, 3 to 4 minutes. Add the broth and season with salt. Bring broth to a boil. Cover the skillet with the lid slightly askew, and reduce the heat to low. Simmer stew 40 to 50 minutes, or until the veal is tender. Set aside.

3. If using fresh peas, cook them in a small saucepan of salted water until tender but still a bit firm to the bite, 2 to 3 minutes depending on size. Drain and set aside. Heat the butter in a small skillet over medium heat. Add the sugar and the vinegar, and stir until the sugar is completely dissolved, less than one minute. Add the cooked fresh or the thawed frozen peas and stir a few times until the peas are well coated with the sauce. Set aside.

4. Add the peas and all of the sauce to the stew. Cook just long enough to mix everything well, less than one minute. Taste, adjust the seasoning, and serve.

Prepare ahead
Through step 2, several hours or a day ahead. Cover and refrigerate.
Through step 3, about 1 hour before your guests arrive.
Complete step 4 just before serving.

TIP: Shiitake mushrooms, grown in China and Japan, are widely used in Oriental cooking. Until a few years ago, these exotic mushrooms were available only from the Orient. Now, they are cultivated in several parts of the United States and are available in many specialized markets across the country. In selecting shiitakes, look for golden brown, firm, meaty mushrooms. If possible, try to use them the same day you buy them. If you need to store them, place them in a large dish in a single layer and cover loosely with a damp kitchen towel. Keep them refrigerated not longer than three or four days. Wipe shiitakes clean with a damp towel just before using.

TIP: When I prepare stews, I double or triple the recipe, then I divide the stew into two or three batches, place them in separate containers and freeze them.

OVEN-BAKED VEAL STEW WITH WHITE WINE AND ARTICHOKES

Stew is one of those dishes in which relatively inexpensive meat and some vegetables can be transformed into a great meal. A bit of wine, broth, lemon peel, and most of all, slow, loving, cooking, and this dish is transformed into a meal fit for a king.

This is a light, delicate stew, with a meltingly tender consistency. It begins on top of the stove and is finished in the oven. As with most stews, it tastes even better if it sits overnight.

¹/₂ pound small artichokes	**4 to 5 fresh sage leaves, chopped, or ¹/₂ teaspoon crumbled dry sage**
3 tablespoons olive oil	
1 pound veal shoulder or stewing veal, cut into 2-inch pieces	**1 cup dry white wine**
	1¹/₂ to 2 cups chicken broth
¹/₃ cup all-purpose flour	**Salt and freshly ground pepper**
	1 tablespoon chopped fresh parsley
¹/₂ medium onion, diced	**Grated peel of ¹/₂ lemon**

1. Prepare the artichokes as instructed on page 91 and set aside until ready to use.

2. Preheat the oven to 350°F. Heat the oil in an ovenproof skillet over medium-high heat. Place the veal in a large colander over a bowl and add the flour. Shake the colander to evenly distribute the flour. Add the veal to the skillet and brown on all sides, 5 to 6 minutes. (Make sure not to crowd the skillet or the veal will not brown evenly.) Scoop up the browned veal with a slotted spoon, drain it against the side of the skillet and transfer it to a plate.

3. Add the onion and the sage to the skillet and cook, stirring, until the onion is pale yellow, 4 to 5 minutes. Return the veal to the pan, raise the heat to high, and add the wine. Cook and stir until the wine is reduced by half, 3 to 4 minutes. Add the broth and season with salt and pepper. Cover the skillet loosely with aluminum foil, and place in the oven. Cook for 30 to 35 minutes, and then add the artichokes. Cook 15 to 20 minutes longer until the meat is tender and the sauce has a nice thick consistency. Add a bit more broth if sauce reduces too much. Stir the stew a few times during cooking.

4. Stir in parsley and grated lemon peel. Taste, adjust the seasoning, and serve hot.

Prepare ahead
Through step 3, several hours or a day ahead. Cover and refrigerate.
Reheat and complete step 4 just before serving.

CRÊPES CANNELLONI WITH RICOTTA AND SMOKED HAM

Crêpes are simple to prepare and are extremely versatile. In this dish, the crêpes take the place of the pasta and become the shells of a delicious filling. Crêpes can be prepared several days or several weeks ahead. Keep them tightly wrapped in the refrigerator or in the freezer. The filling can also be used to stuff ready-made pasta, such as large shells or large rigatoni.

For the Crêpes

2 large eggs

¹/₂ cup milk

¹/₂ cup all-purpose flour

4 tablespoons unsalted butter, melted and cooled

For the Filling

¹/₂ pound ricotta

¹/₄ pound thinly sliced smoked ham, finely diced

³/₄ cup freshly grated Parmigiano-Reggiano

1 large egg, lightly beaten

¹/₄ teaspoon grated nutmeg

2 tablespoons chopped fresh parsley

Salt

2 to 3 tablespoons unsalted butter, melted

For the Tomato-Cream Sauce

1 tablespoon unsalted butter

2 cups canned plum tomatoes with their juice, put through a food mill to remove the seeds

2 to 3 tablespoons heavy cream

Salt

1. *Prepare the Crêpes:* Put the eggs, milk, flour, and 1 tablespoon of the melted butter in the bowl of a food processor and process until smooth. Transfer batter to a bowl and let it rest for about one hour. (Batter can also be assembled in a bowl and whisked until smooth.)

2. Heat an 8-inch crêpe pan or nonstick skillet on medium-high heat and brush with some of the melted butter. When butter begins to smoke, pour just enough batter in the pan to cover the bottom lightly. Tilt and rotate the pan immediately to spread the batter evenly. After 30 to 40 seconds, when the top of the crêpe begins to solidify and small bubbles appear on the surface, check the bottom of the crêpe, which should be lightly golden. Turn the crêpe over with a spatula and cook 15 to 20 seconds longer. Place the crêpe on a flat dish and proceed to cook the other crêpes. Stack them as they are done and cool completely. (Place a small sheet of wax paper between each crêpe if they stick together.)

3. *Prepare the filling:* In a small bowl thoroughly combine ricotta, ham, $^1/_3$ cup of the Parmigiano, egg, nutmeg, and parsley, and season with salt.

4. Preheat the oven to 400°F. Butter a baking dish large enough to fit cannelloni in one layer.

5. Lay crêpes on a work surface and place 1 to 2 heaping tablespoons of the filling horizontally in the center of each crêpe. Fold crêpes over filling to make cannelloni. Place them in the buttered baking dish, brush lightly with melted butter, and sprinkle generously with remaining Parmigiano.

6. *Prepare the Tomato Cream Sauce:* Heat 1 tablespoon of the butter in a small saucepan over medium heat. Add the tomatoes and cook 5 to 6 minutes stirring occasionally. Add the cream and season with salt. Let the sauce bubble a few more minutes, then reduce the heat to very low. Keep the sauce warm while you bake the cannelloni.

7. Put the baking dish on the middle level of the oven, and bake until the cheese is melted and has a light golden color, 6 to 8 minutes.

8. Spoon some sauce in the center of two flat serving dishes and swirl the sauce around to cover the bottom. Place cannelloni in the center of each dish and serve at once.

Prepare ahead

Through step 6, several hours or one day ahead. Refrigerate. Reheat the sauce gently at the time of serving. If preparing ahead, do not preheat oven in step 4 until ready to bake. Complete steps 7 and 8 just before serving.

LOVING DINNERS FOR TWO

Vegetables

Glazed Julienne of Carrots

Swiss Chard with Raisins, Pine Nuts, and Lemon

Buttered New Potatoes with Walnut Pesto

Gratin of Potatoes, Leeks, and Cheese

Baked Tomatoes Stuffed with Rice, Olives, and Capers

GLAZED JULIENNE OF CARROTS

2 medium carrots, peeled and cut into very thin strips

1 tablespoon unsalted butter

1 tablespoon sugar

1 to 2 tablespoons lemon juice

$1/4$ cup golden raisins, soaked in 1 cup of water for 20 minutes, then drained

2 tablespoons pine nuts

Salt

1. Bring a small saucepan of water to a boil over medium-high heat. Add carrots and cook just enough to soften. (They should still have a crunchy consistency.) Drain carrots and rinse under cold running water to stop the cooking. Set aside until ready to use.

2. Melt the butter in a medium skillet over medium heat. Add sugar, lemon juice, raisins, and pine nuts. Stir a few times until sugar is dissolved. Add carrots, season with salt, and remove from heat.

3. Just before serving, put the skillet back on medium heat and stir carrots a few times until they are coated with the sugar/lemon mixture. Serve hot.

Prepare ahead
Through step 2, one hour or so ahead.
Complete step 3 just before serving.

I never worry about diets. The only carrots that interest me are
the number you get in a diamond.
—Mae West

SWISS CHARD WITH RAISINS, PINE NUTS, AND LEMON

1 bunch Swiss chard	**1 to 2 tablespoons olive oil**
Salt	**2 garlic cloves, peeled**
$^1/_3$ cup pine nuts	**Juice of 1 small lemon**
$^1/_3$ cup golden raisins, soaked in 1 cup of lukewarm water for 20 minutes and drained	**Freshly ground pepper**

1. Remove and discard stems from the Swiss chard. Wash leaves thoroughly under cold running water to remove any grit.

2. Bring a medium saucepan of water to a boil over medium heat. Add 1 teaspoon of salt and the chard. Cook, uncovered, 7 to 8 minutes, or until chard is tender. Drain chard well and set aside.

3. Place pine nuts in a small baking dish and roast them in a preheated 400°F oven until lightly golden, 3 to 4 minutes.

4. Heat the oil in a medium skillet over medium heat. Add the garlic cloves and brown on all sides. Discard the garlic.

5. Add the cooked chard, pine nuts, raisins, and lemon juice to the skillet, and season with salt and pepper. Turn the heat to medium-low and stir for 1 to 2 minutes to heat the chard through and to coat it with the flavored oil. Serve at once.

Prepare ahead
Through step 3, several hours ahead.
Complete steps 4 and 5 just before serving.

BUTTERED NEW POTATOES WITH WALNUT PESTO

In using pesto, keep in mind that only a bit of this aromatic sauce is needed to dress pasta or vegetables. Too much pesto will overpower the dish. Pesto sauce should always be served uncooked. Heating pesto destroys its freshness and fragrance. When pairing pesto with pasta or vegetables, always stir it together quickly, off the heat, so that pesto will retain both its fragrance and its beautiful green color.

$^1/_3$ **cup shelled walnuts**

2 cups loosely packed fresh basil leaves

2 garlic cloves

$^1/_3$ **to** $^1/_2$ **cup olive oil**

Salt

$^1/_3$ **cup freshly grated Parmigiano-Reggiano**

$^1/_2$ **pound red new potatoes with skin on, left whole if small, cut in half if large**

1 tablespoon unsalted butter

1. *Prepare pesto sauce:* Chop walnuts finely in a food processor. Add basil, garlic, and olive oil, and season lightly with salt. Process until smooth. Put pesto in a small bowl and stir in the Parmigiano. Taste and adjust the seasoning. Reserve two tablespoons of pesto for the potatoes, then cover the bowl with plastic wrap and refrigerate or freeze remaining pesto. *(Makes about $^3/_4$ cup pesto.)*

2. *Prepare potatoes:* Bring a medium pot of water to a boil over medium-high heat. Add the potatoes and cook, uncovered, until tender, 10 to 12 minutes. Drain and set aside.

3. Heat the butter in a medium skillet over medium heat. Add the potatoes and season lightly with salt. Stir a few times until potatoes are coated with the butter and are heated all the way through. Remove skillet from heat and add the 2 tablespoons of reserved pesto sauce. Stir quickly and serve with roasted, grilled, or baked meat or fowl.

Prepare ahead
Pesto sauce, step 1, can be prepared several hours or a few days ahead.
Boil potatoes, step 2, several hours ahead.
Complete step 3 just before serving.

TIP: Freeze pesto without the addition of Parmigiano. Stir the cheese into the pesto just before using for a fresher taste and more interesting texture. Pesto can be kept frozen for several months.

GRATIN OF POTATOES, LEEKS, AND CHEESE

"Gratin" dishes are great to prepare for two or 20, since they can be assembled way ahead of time and baked at the last moment. This potato gratin obviously serves more than two people. Rejoice, since the day after, the leftovers will be only for you! It can be served as an appetizer, a luncheon entrée, or as a side dish to a roasted or grilled entrée.

4 baking potatoes (about 1^1/$_2$ pounds), peeled and sliced into ^{1}/$_4$-inch thick rounds

2 tablespoons olive oil

4 to 5 leeks, white part only, thinly sliced and thoroughly washed

Butter for baking dish

^{1}/$_2$ cup plain bread crumbs

Salt

^{1}/$_4$ pound Swiss cheese, coarsely grated or minced

2 tablespoons unsalted butter, melted

^{1}/$_4$ cup freshly grated Parmigiano-Reggiano

1. Bring a medium saucepan of salted water to a boil over medium-high heat. Add the potatoes and cook, uncovered, until they are tender but still a bit firm to the bite, 8 to 10 minutes. Drain potatoes and set aside.

2. Heat the oil in a medium skillet over medium heat. Add the leeks and cook, stirring, until lightly golden and soft, 6 to 7 minutes. With a slotted spoon transfer leeks to a dish.

3. Preheat the oven to 375°F. Butter the bottom and sides of an 8-inch baking dish and coat with half of the bread crumbs. Place half of the potatoes in the dish in one layer, overlapping them slightly, and season with salt. Top potatoes with leeks and sprinkle Swiss cheese over leeks. Top cheese with the remaining potatoes and brush them generously with the melted butter. Season with salt and sprinkle Parmigiano and remaining bread crumbs over potatoes.

4. Bake for 20 to 25 minutes, or until potatoes are golden brown. Serve warm. *Makes one, 8-inch gratin of potatoes.*

Prepare ahead
Through step 3, several hours ahead.
The baking, step 4, can be done just before serving, or about one hour ahead.
If baked ahead, briefly reheat the gratin in the oven at the time of serving.

BAKED TOMATOES STUFFED WITH RICE, OLIVES, AND CAPERS

This dish is also delicious with uncooked tomatoes. Cook the rice and assemble with the olives, capers, parsley, etc. Empty tomato cavities and drain them on paper towels. Stuff tomatoes and serve at room temperature.

$^1/_3$ **cup short grain rice**	**8 pitted green olives, quartered**
2 large firm ripe tomatoes	**1 tablespoon capers, rinsed**
Salt and freshly ground pepper	**1 tablespoon chopped fresh parsley**
2 tablespoons olive oil	
2 tablespoons minced white onions	

1. Bring a small saucepan of water to a boil over medium heat. Add the rice and cook until tender but still firm, 8 to 10 minutes. Drain, place in a bowl and set aside.

2. Slice off $^1/_3$ of the tomato tops. With a small knife, remove the seeds and the inside pulp, leaving the tomatoes with a hollow cavity. Dice the pulp of the tomatoes and add to the rice. Season tomato cavity with salt and pepper, and turn them upside down on paper towels to drain.

3. Heat 1 tablespoon of the oil in a small skillet over medium heat. Add the onion and cook, stirring, until lightly golden, 3 to 4 minutes. Scoop up the onion with a slotted spoon and add to the rice. Add olives, capers, parsley, and remaining oil and season with salt and pepper. Fill tomato cavities with the rice and place in a baking dish.

4. Preheat the oven to 325°F. Cover tomatoes loosely with foil to prevent rice from becoming crunchy, and bake until tomatoes and rice are heated through and the tomato skins barely begin to shrivel, 8 to 10 minutes. Serve warm.

Prepare ahead
Through step 3, several hours ahead.
Complete step 4 just before serving.

LOVING DINNERS FOR TWO

Desserts

Baked Peaches with Crème Anglaise

Poached Pears with Hot Chocolate Sauce

White Chocolate Mousse with Brandy

Chilled Chocolate Soufflé

Deep Dish Apple Pie with Plum Jam and Raisins

Mint-Lemon Mousse

Crêpes with Cherry Compote

Strawberry Sorbet

Basic Pastry Dough (Paté Brisée)

BAKED PEACHES WITH CRÈME ANGLAISE

Crème Anglaise is a flourless, light custard sauce that pairs very well with all kinds of fresh or baked fruit. It is probably one of the easiest sauces to prepare and certainly one of the most delicious. In winter, use it over baked apples or pears.

For the Peaches

2 tablespoons sliced almonds

1 tablespoon sugar

1 tablespoon melted butter

1 tablespoon Grand Marnier, brandy, or cognac

2 large, ripe peaches, washed and halved, with pits removed

For the Crème Anglaise

3 large egg yolks

1/4 cup sugar

3/4 cup milk, heated just short of boiling

2 tablespoons Grand Marnier, brandy, or cognac

1. Preheat the oven to 400°F. Toast the almonds until lightly golden. Chop almonds into fine pieces and transfer to a small bowl. Stir in the sugar, melted butter, and 1 tablespoon Grand Marnier. Put the peach halves in a small buttered baking dish, and fill each cavity with the almond mixture. Bake 15 to 20 minutes, or until peaches can be pierced easily with a thin knife. Set aside to cool.

2. *Prepare Crème Anglaise:* Combine the egg yolks with sugar in a small saucepan. Beat with a wire whisk until the mixture turns pale yellow and thick, 2 to 3 minutes. Drizzle hot milk into the egg yolks a bit at a time, and mix with a wooden spoon to combine. (Do not beat milk with a wire whisk, or mixture will become foamy.) Put the saucepan over low heat and cook, stirring constantly with a wooden spoon, until cream coats the back of the spoon, 5 to 6 minutes. (Do not let cream get to a fast simmer, or you will cook the eggs.) Transfer to a bowl and stir in Grand Marnier. Cool to room temperature.

3. Just before serving, spoon *crème anglaise* into two serving dishes and swirl lightly to coat the bottom of the dish completely. Put the peaches on top of the sauce and serve.

Prepare ahead
Through step 2, several hours ahead. Cover and refrigerate.
Step 3, just before serving.

POACHED PEARS WITH CHOCOLATE SAUCE

For the Pears

2 large Bosc pears

Juice of 1 lemon

2 to 3 cups dry white wine

$^1/_3$ cup sugar

Grated peel of 1 lemon

For the Chocolate Sauce

$^1/_2$ cup heavy cream

4 ounces semisweet baking chocolate squares, cut into small pieces

1. *Prepare the pears*: Peel the pears, but leave the stems attached. Cut off a small slice from bottom of pears so they will stand up evenly. Brush pears with lemon juice.

2. Put the pears in a medium saucepan with the wine, sugar, and grated lemon peel. Bring to a gentle boil over moderate heat. Reduce the heat to low and cover the pan. Simmer until pears are tender and can be pierced easily with a thin knife, 20 to 25 minutes. Baste pears a few times during cooking. Remove from heat and cool pears in the poaching liquid. Set aside until ready to use.

3. *Prepare the chocolate sauce*: Put the cream and chocolate in the top part of a double boiler. Place the top part of the double boiler over the bottom of the double boiler containing a few inches of simmering water. Stir the chocolate as it melts. When completely melted, turn off the heat, cover, and keep chocolate warm until ready to use.

4. Place pears on serving dishes, spoon warm chocolate sauce over them, and serve.

Prepare ahead

Through step 2, several hours ahead or overnight. Cover and refrigerate.
Through step 3, several hours ahead. When ready to serve, reheat the chocolate sauce gently over simmering water, or in a microwave oven.
Complete step 4 just before serving.

TIP: Save syrup from cooking the pears. Freeze and use another time.

WHITE CHOCOLATE MOUSSE WITH BRANDY

Alice Medrich, author of the splendid book, "Cocolat" and noted national authority on chocolate writes "Legally, there is no such thing as white chocolate, because in this country, nothing can be called 'chocolate' unless it contains chocolate 'liqueur,'—the pulverized roasted cocoa bean consisting of cocoa butter and cocoa solids. Technically, it must be called 'white confectionery coating.' The problem is that there are two types of white confectionery coating, both informally called white chocolate. Only one of them, however, contains cocoa butter, preferably as its 'only' fat. I strongly believe that this latter type should be allowed legal distinction of being called 'white chocolate.' The other type of confectionery coating is made with vegetable fats instead of cocoa butter, so it bears no relation whatsoever to the cocoa bean."

$1/4$ pound white chocolate	**2 tablespoons sugar**
2 tablespoons brandy, cognac, or Grand Marnier	**$3/4$ cup heavy cream, beaten to a medium-firm consistency**
$1/2$ teaspoon vanilla extract	**Fresh raspberries**
1 large egg	**Shaved dark chocolate**

1. Break the chocolate into very small pieces and place, along with the brandy and vanilla extract, into a medium bowl or in the top part of a double boiler. Set bowl or top part of double boiler over two inches of very gently simmering water and stir several times, until chocolate has melted. Set aside to cool.

2. Beat the egg with the sugar in a small bowl until it has doubled in volume. Fold the egg into the melted chocolate. Fold the whipped cream a bit at a time into the melted chocolate until thoroughly incorporated and smooth. Spoon mousse into serving glasses, cover, and refrigerate for several hours or overnight.

3. Just before serving, decorate each mousse with some fresh berries or shaved dark chocolate.

Prepare ahead
Through step 2, several hours or a day ahead.
Complete step 3 just before serving.

TIP: Alice's tips for buying white chocolate follow: "Beware of white chocolate that is too inexpensive. Read the label carefully to be sure you are buying white chocolate that is made with cocoa butter. Store excess chocolate in the freezer. Frozen chocolate should be thawed completely without unwrapping."

CHILLED CHOCOLATE SOUFFLÉ

If you are a chocolate lover, this dish is for you. This dark, rich, chilled soufflé is quintessentially simple to prepare, provided you follow the simple steps on how to melt chocolate properly.

Keep in mind that chocolate in general, and white chocolate in particular, burns easily if allowed to melt over high heat. Make sure the water in the double boiler is at the gentlest of simmers. Stir frequently to facilitate the melting. Chocolate must be cooled before it is combined with the other ingredients.

4 ounces bittersweet chocolate

2 tablespoons Grand Marnier or brandy

1 tablespoon water

2 large egg yolks at room temperature, lightly beaten in a small bowl

2 large egg whites, beaten with a pinch of cream of tartar and 1 tablespoon sugar, to a medium-stiff consistency

Whipped cream or fresh berries for garnish

1. Break the chocolate into several small pieces, and place in a medium bowl or in the top part of a double boiler with the Grand Marnier and the water. Set bowl or top part of double boiler over two inches of gently simmering water and stir several times until chocolate has melted. Set aside to cool.

2. Whisk egg yolks gently into chocolate mixture. Thoroughly fold $1/3$ of the beaten egg whites into the cool chocolate to soften it, then fold in remaining egg whites. Pour into six-ounce soufflé bowls and refrigerate until ready to use.

Prepare ahead
Through step 2, several hours or a day ahead.
Just before serving, garnish with whipped cream or a few fresh berries.

TIP: Some good, suggested chocolate brands are *Callebaut, Nestlé,* and *Tobler.* Check with your specialty food store.

DEEP-DISH APPLE PIE WITH PLUM JAM AND RAISINS

For these pies, use any ovenproof bowls, soufflé dishes or ramekins you have in the house. This will give the dish your own personalized look.

1 recipe **Basic Pastry Dough (see page 75)**

3 large **golden delicious or Granny Smith apples, peeled, cored, and thinly sliced**

$^1/_2$ cup **plum jam**

$^1/_4$ cup **sugar**

$^1/_3$ cup **golden raisins, soaked for 20 minutes in warm water and drained**

2 tablespoons **unsalted butter, cut into small pieces**

1 large **egg, lightly beaten with one teaspoon of water**

1. Prepare the Basic Pastry Dough. Shape it into a ball, and refrigerate for one hour.

2. Preheat the oven to 400°F. Butter two 10-ounce soufflé dishes.

3. In a medium bowl, combine the apples, jam, sugar, and raisins, and mix well.

4. On a lightly-floured surface, roll out half the dough into a 16-inch, thin sheet. Cut the sheet into two, 8-inch rounds. Line the soufflé dishes, allowing the excess dough to go over the sides. Press the dough gently to fit into the dishes evenly. Pile the apple mixture into the dishes and dot with butter.

5. Roll out the remaining dough to make two additional circles large enough to completely cover the apples. Press the top and bottom dough together and trim any excess. Fold dough over to form a border and pinch together to seal. Brush the dough with the beaten egg, and prick the tops of the pies with a fork in several places to allow steam to escape while baking.

6. If you want to make an apple and leaf decoration, shape the apple and leaves from the dough scraps with a sharp knife. Using a beaten egg or ice water, paste the apple and leaves over the pies.

◀ Deep-Dish Apple Pie with Plum Jam and Raisins

7.   Bake 30 to 40 minutes or until the crust is golden brown. Cool to room temperature and serve. *Makes two deep-dish apple pies, baked in 10-ounce soufflé dishes.*

Prepare ahead
Through step 7, several hours ahead.
If you plan to serve the pies warm instead of room temperature, put them back in the oven briefly, just before serving.

Whether the feast lasts for 7 years or whether it lasts for a week or a night, and whether we have forgotten the abundance and nature of the fare and the colour of the wine, and whether the faces of the company are clear as they then were, or are blurred, we still feel we have taken part in a unique event.
—Patience Gray

MINT-LEMON MOUSSE

Fresh mint gives the mousse its unique character. If fresh mint is unavailable, increase the amount of lemon juice or the crème de menthe. Then, obviously, the name of the mousse will change to "lemon mousse" or "mousse with crème de menthe." See how easy it is to create new dishes?

$1/3$ cup loosely packed fresh mint leaves, finely minced

1 cup heavy cream

1 teaspoon unflavored gelatin

$1/3$ cup hot water

$1/3$ cup sugar

Juice of 1 lemon

1 to 2 tablespoons crème de menthe liqueur

2 large egg whites, stiffly beaten with 2 tablespoons sugar

Fresh mint leaves or fresh berries to garnish

1. In a small bowl, combine the mint with $1/2$ cup of the cream and refrigerate covered for 2 to 3 hours to blend flavors.

2. In another small bowl, stir gelatin into boiling water until dissolved. Cool to room temperature.

3. Put mint and cream in a blender or food processor and process until smooth. Transfer mixture to the bowl of an electric mixer, add remaining cream and sugar, and beat until stiff. Add lemon juice, crème de menthe, and cooled gelatin. Beat at low speed briefly to mix. Fold in egg whites thoroughly.

4. Put mixture into a pastry bag and squeeze into large dessert glasses. Cover and refrigerate several hours or overnight. Just before serving, decorate mousse with a sprig or two of fresh mint or sprinkle some fresh berries over the top.

Prepare ahead
Through step 4, several hours or a day ahead.

CRÊPES WITH CHERRY COMPOTE

If you have never made crêpes in your life, chances are that the first batch will be less than perfect. Some will be thin, some thick, and some will have odd shapes. Do not worry; after a few minutes, you will get the hang of it. Crêpes are extremely versatile. They can be served with savory fillings as appetizers, first courses, entrées, and, of course, as desserts.

1 Basic Crêpe recipe (see page 55)

³/₄ pound fresh sweet cherries pitted, or 2 cups frozen cherries (see Tip)

1 cup medium-bodied red wine

Grated peel of 1 lemon

¹/₄ cup fresh lemon juice

¹/₃ cup sugar

1 tablespoon unsalted butter

1 to 2 tablespoons cherry preserves

1 to 2 tablespoons additional sugar for topping the crêpes

1. Prepare the Crêpes as instructed on page 55, and set aside.

2. Prepare the cherry compote: Combine cherries, wine, lemon peel, lemon juice, sugar, and butter in a small saucepan. Bring to a boil over medium heat. Reduce the heat to low and simmer 10 to 15 minutes until the liquid is almost all reduced. Stir a few times during cooking. Add the cherry preserves and cook 2 to 3 minutes longer. At this point, the sauce should be a thick glaze and should thoroughly coat the cherries. Transfer cherries to a bowl and cool.

3. Arrange crêpes on a flat surface and add one to two tablespoons of cherry compote on one half of each crêpe. Fold the empty half of the crêpe over the filling, then fold again, loosely, to form a triangle. Place the crêpes in a buttered baking dish and set aside until ready to use.

4. Preheat the oven to 400°F. Sprinkle crêpes with sugar and bake in the middle level of the oven until sugar begins to caramelize and the tops of the crêpes turn lightly golden, 4 to 5 minutes. Serve at once.

Prepare ahead

Prepare crêpes in step 1, several hours or several days ahead, and keep refrigerated until ready to use. (Crêpes can also be frozen for several weeks.)

Prepare the cherry compote in step 2 several hours ahead, and keep refrigerated until ready to use.

Assemble the crêpes in step 3 a few hours ahead.

Bake the crêpes, step 4, just before serving.

TIP: If using frozen cherries, thaw the cherries and drain the juice. Simmer the wine with the lemon juice, lemon peel, sugar, and butter until wine is almost all reduced and sauce is thick and bubbling. Add the cherries and the cherry preserves to the pan and simmer for a few minutes until the cherry mixture is thick and glazy. Transfer cherry mixture to a bowl and chill for one hour. Proceed as instructed in step 3 of the recipe.

STRAWBERRY SORBET

Freshly made sorbet has a soft, smooth, velvety consistency. Ideally, sorbet and ice cream should be served shortly after they are made. If you must freeze your sorbet after you have made it, let it soften in the refrigerator for about 15 minutes before serving it.

1 cup sugar	**4 tablespoons lemon juice**
1 cup water	**1 large egg white at room temperature, beaten with 2 tablespoons of sugar until medium stiff**
2 pints strawberries, washed and hulled	

1. *Prepare the syrup:* In a small saucepan, combine the sugar and water and bring to a gentle boil over medium heat. Cook, stirring, until sugar is completely dissolved, about 2 minutes. Cool to room temperature.

2. *Complete the dish:* Put strawberries and lemon juice in a food processor fitted with the metal blade and process until smooth. Put puréed strawberries through a sieve into a large bowl and stir in cooled syrup. (Makes about 3 cups puréed strawberries.)

3. Put strawberry mixture in the bowl of an ice cream machine, and process, following manufacturer's directions, for about 20 minutes. Add the egg white and run the ice cream machine until sorbet is ready. Serve in chilled glasses. *Makes about 1 quart.*

Prepare ahead
Through step 3, several hours or a day ahead.

BASIC PASTRY DOUGH (PATÉ BRISÉE)

This is a basic pastry dough recipe. Once you have the right proportions of butter, flour, and liquid, making a perfect pastry dough with a moist, pliable consistency is a snap. Make sure to follow the recipe precisely and have all your ingredients well chilled. Do not overwork the dough or the butter will heat up, making it too soft and sticky. Simply gather the dough lightly into a ball. The dough must be refrigerated at least one hour to facilitate the rolling. If dough is very firm after it has been refrigerated for several hours or overnight, leave it to soften a bit for a few minutes at room temperature before rolling it out. Pastry dough can also be frozen.

2 cups all-purpose unbleached flour

2 tablespoons sugar

1 stick plus 2 tablespoons cold, unsalted butter, cut into small pieces

1 large egg, lightly beaten in a small bowl

¼ to ⅓ cup chilled white wine

Makes two, 8- to 10-inch tarts or one, 8- to 10-inch double crust pie

Making pastry dough in a food processor

1. Put the flour, sugar, and butter in the bowl of a food processor fitted with the metal blade. Pulse the machine on and off until the butter is combined with the flour and the mixture has a coarse, granular consistency. (The granular consistency comes from the butter, which, in retaining a bit of chunkiness, will give the pastry a nice, flaky texture.) Add the egg and pulse the machine. Add the wine a bit at a time through the feed tube until the dough is loosely gathered around the blade, is moist, and holds together easily.

2. Gather the dough on a floured work surface and shape lightly into a ball. Flatten the dough with the palm of your hand, dust it with flour, and wrap in plastic wrap. Refrigerate at least one hour.

Making pastry dough by hand

1. Put the flour, sugar, and butter in a large bowl and combine, rubbing mixture between the palms of your hands, until it has a coarse granular consistency. Add the egg, sugar, and wine, and mix everything well with your hands until the dough is moist and holds together easily.

2. Put dough on a floured work surface and shape lightly into a ball. Flatten the dough lightly with the palm of your hand, dust it with flour, and wrap in plastic wrap. Refrigerate at least one hour.

LOVING DINNERS FOR FRIENDS

"It is a fact of life that people give dinner parties, and when they invite you, you have to turn around and invite them back. Often they retaliate by inviting you again, and you must then extend another invitation. Back and forth you go, like ping-pong balls, and what you end up with is called a social life.
—Laurie Colwin

THE CARE AND FEEDING OF FRIENDS

Philosophers through time, from Plato, Aristotle, Cicero, St. Francis, Thomas More, and Adam Smith to Bertrand Russell and Andre Maurois all recognized the great reciprocal benefits intrinsic in friendships and wrote inspiring treatises on the subject. They suggest that it may not be love that makes the world go 'round, but friendship. Few of us would disagree. Many of us have recognized the true value of friendship only after we have lost it. We have learned, too late, that friendship is a very frail plant and, like love, dies without skilled maintenance. In fact, it has been suggested that friendships demand infinitely more than love.

It is a real tragedy that some of us seem unwilling to take the time or put forth the energy required to enrich our friendships. We fall back on weak excuses such as lack of time, busy schedules, or the mobility of our achievement-oriented society as the basic villains that prevent us from seeking and maintaining friendships. Of course, by so doing, we conveniently exonerate ourselves of any responsibility. We then wonder why we are lonely or why our lives seem to lack spontaneity and excitement.

I learned a great deal about the importance of friendships when I was growing up. My parents had a very large circle of close friends, mostly poor and all with large families. There were those, like themselves, who had recently immigrated to this country and were inextricably tied together by mores and shared memories of the "Old Country." To this core group they eagerly added new friends, neighbors, and coworkers, an endless mix of personalities and cultures.

Nothing was ever too good, too inconvenient, or too troublesome for these friends. In fact, Mama and Papa always seemed to be involved in some elaborate plan to bring them all together. These plans, inevitably, ended up focusing upon food, which meant that the family was frequently to be found scurrying about in joyful anticipation, preparing for the exciting occasions. The preparation was often as much fun as the planned function itself and would commence days in advance and continue until the first guest arrived on the appointed day.

Our dining room table would seat eight and could be expanded to comfortably seat 12, but this was never enough. Saw horses connected with huge wooden planks were needed to accommodate all the friends invited. Of course, room could always be made for the drop-ins. No problem. The more the merrier. "You have to eat. So why not here with friends? We have plenty for everyone! So sit down and eat!" Mama would say.

Along with the aromas and the visual stimulation, I have an auditory memory of these happy times as well; the clatter of dishes, voices raised animatedly, the gleeful cries of children, glasses touched in toasts, and lips smacked in exclamations of gastronomic delectation and delight. There was a certain lunacy about these groups, which continually led to unrestrained eruptions of laughter—the perfect agent for bringing us all closer in a mellifluous, melodious *Symphonie Gastronomique!*

Even the clean-up was a clinking-clanking chorale. Since mechanical dishwashers were unheard of at that time, a human assembly line was created: one person clearing the table, another scraping the dishes, someone rinsing, another washing, several drying, all to the rhythm of conversation, laughter, and song. The kitchen was surely the place to be!

These friendly gatherings usually lasted late into the night. Time had no meaning as stories were told, dreams shared, and hopes revealed. It was always a shock when one of our friends rose, as if from a trance, to announce that the hour was late. Suddenly there was activity everywhere as children were gathered up in varying states of fussiness, frustration, or fatigue. Coats were reclaimed and a mass exodus ensued. These last moments created a crescendo of appreciation for the quality of the dinner, always spiced with spontaneous hugs and kisses. These evenings remain indelibly etched in my mind and heart.

In a world that so often seems full of uncertainty and marginal values, having friends offers us something we can count on. Friends constitute a solid part of our lives. They feed our spirits, our senses, our minds and hearts in mutual enhancement. In truth, we don't discover ourselves by ourselves. We find who we are in interaction with close significant others. The Latin word for friendship, *amicitia,* is derived from the word for love, *amor.* Understandably so, since love is the prime ingredient of friendships.

Friendship is a choice, a gift, a universal characteristic of human society. It is the gift that keeps on giving. I would be nothing without my friends.

I was born and raised in East Los Angeles. There could not have been a better place to grow up at the time. It was a small community on the outskirts of The City of Angels, enriched and made more exciting by diverse ethnic groups: Jewish, Mexican, Italian and Japanese. Most of our neighbors, like ourselves, were immigrants, and the term "melting pot" was most appropriate for us, not only in its sociological sense, but literally in the diverse cuisines. We were always inviting neighbors to eat with us, and as is usually the case, invitations were reciprocated. So, tacos, potato latkes, sauerkraut, and miso soup were no surprise to us. Our friends, in turn, were treated to Mama's pasta and Papa's risotto. It was food that bridged our diversity, and it was food that kept us united over the years in loving friendship.

Though there are many possibilities for celebrating our friends, I think the most appealing and fruitful source of contentment and reassurance is sharing a home-cooked meal with them. It is a way of giving that special gift of self, sharing through our personality and creativity, something for them alone.

There is a special feeling of good will that descends upon an evening of dining at home with friends. Going to a restaurant is fine, but often leaves something to be desired. When a restaurant meal is over, so is the evening. What a pity, since it is just at this moment that the real enchantment begins. It is most satisfying after the dishes have been cleared, to sit and watch the candles as they flicker and slowly drip; to listen as the once animated conversation slips into a comforting, velvety softness; to smile as the guests languidly play with the remaining crumbs on the tablecloth and savor the last few sips of wine or the rich warmth of their coffee, obviously too peaceful and contented to say goodnight. What a wonderful feeling to know that through our efforts the alchemy of love has worked its magic again, making what was already good into something priceless.

A dinner we plan and prepare is a show of appreciation to those who help us to define ourselves, who give us a feeling of security and well being—small price for such a precious gift. Friendship makes friendship. We cannot help but agree with Robert Louis Stevenson's comment that "Friendship is the gift you give yourself."

Human survival is dependent upon healthy relationships, people interacting in joy and harmony. Therefore, to lose a friend is an irreparable loss and usually occurs because we fail to recognize the time, the work, and the constant nurturing that friendships require. The result of this neglect is often loneliness of our own making. We wonder why life lacks the luster we once knew. We seem to be accumulating fewer memorable memories. There seems to be less to anticipate eagerly. This becomes more apparent as we grow older. We find ourselves yearning for the rewards we once knew, that were most often brought on by our times of human togetherness.

It is certainly true that, in a very real sense, we are all alone. But it is in the process of overcoming this knowledge that we make the effort required to create a "Family of Choice" around us, a group of individuals whom we enjoy, who enhance our lives and enlighten our hours. By so doing, we make our aloneness more bearable. In fact, it is from this knowledge of loneliness that we are motivated to seek love, and from which our love is born.

There are few things in my life that bring as much joy as gathering friends together. I don't need the excuse of an extraordinary situation. In fact, I prefer creating happenings. . .a "making it through another day" celebration, or a "discovery of a new part of yourself" party. Any excuse to celebrate friendships!

If your desire is to communicate love to friends, there isn't a "special time" to express it. You can do it any time, this very second! What a waste to wait for that special moment when the moment is *now*. I had a dear friend who bragged that he had put away a case of a most exquisite wine that he was saving for "an exceptional occasion" with family and friends. He died last year. The wine still stands in wait. Of all the sad expressions one hears in life, perhaps the saddest is, "I could have. . .and I didn't."

LOVING DINNERS FOR FRIENDS

Starters

Shrimp Chowder

Two-Bean Soup

Tortilla Soup with Chiles and Jack Cheese

Pasta Salad with Shrimp, Broccoli,
and Sun-Dried Tomatoes

Baby Artichokes and Potato Salad

Tomato, Mozzarella, and Grilled Bread Salad

Suzette Swordfish Salad with Roasted Onion
and Tomatoes

Orange, Fennel, and Radicchio Salad

Bruschetta with Fresh Tomatoes and Grilled Eggplant

Eggplant Caponata

SHRIMP CHOWDER

If at all possible, make this dish with the Basic Fish Broth, because it will give this soup a taste that canned clam juice will not be able to match.

2 tablespoons olive oil	1 tablespoon minced chives
1 tablespoon unsalted butter	$1/2$ teaspoon chili pepper flakes (optional)
1 small yellow onion, diced	
1 medium leek (white part only), diced	1 cup dry white wine
	6 cups Basic Fish Broth (see page 42) or canned clam juice
2 medium boiling potatoes, peeled and diced	Salt
2 celery stalks, diced	1 pound medium shrimp, peeled, deveined, and diced
1 red bell pepper, seeded and diced	$1/4$ cup heavy cream
1 garlic clove, minced	1 tablespoon chopped fresh parsley

1. Heat the oil and butter in a large saucepan over medium heat. Add onion and leek. Cook, stirring, until the onion is pale yellow, 4 to 5 minutes. Add potatoes, celery, bell pepper, garlic, chives, and pepper flakes (if using). Cook, stirring for a few minutes.

2. Raise the heat to high and add the wine. Cook, stirring, until wine is almost all reduced. Add broth and bring to a boil. Reduce the heat to low, and simmer, uncovered, 30 to 40 minutes. Stir a few times during cooking. Season with salt.

3. Put the soup in a food processor or blender and process until smooth. Strain the soup through a sieve back into the saucepan and bring to a gentle boil. Add the shrimp and cream, and simmer, uncovered, 5 to 6 minutes, stirring a few times. Just before serving, stir in the parsley. *Makes 6 servings.*

Prepare ahead
Through step 3, a few hours ahead. Cover and refrigerate.
When ready to serve, reheat the soup over low heat.

TWO-BEAN SOUP

For centuries, dried beans have been a staple in many countries because they are economical and highly nutritious. Today, their popularity has increased by leaps and bounds because of the high interest in vegetarian cooking and the decrease in the consumption of meat. Dried beans are widely available in most supermarkets, and the lesser known, such as cannellini beans, can be found in specialized food stores or Italian markets.

This delicious, hearty soup becomes thicker and denser as it sits. If prepared a day ahead, you might need to thin it with a bit of additional broth at the time of serving.

1 cup dried cranberry beans, sorted and rinsed

1 cup dried cannellini beans or white kidney beans, sorted and rinsed

$^1/_3$ cup olive oil, preferably extra-virgin

1 medium onion, minced

2 garlic cloves, minced

5 to 6 fresh large sage leaves, chopped, or 2 dried sage leaves, crumbled

2 tablespoons chopped fresh rosemary, or 1 teaspoon chopped dry rosemary

$2^1/_2$ quarts (10 cups) chicken broth

Salt and freshly ground pepper

2 tablespoons chopped fresh parsley

Olive oil to drizzle over the soup

1. Put the cranberry and cannellini beans in two separate large bowls and cover with cold water. Soak the beans overnight. Drain and rinse thoroughly.

2. Put the cranberry beans in a medium saucepan and cover with cold water 2 inches above the beans. Bring the water to a gentle boil and simmer about 1 to $1^1/_2$ hours, or until the beans are tender. (Cranberry beans will take longer to cook than white beans.) With a slotted spoon, transfer cranberry beans to a food processor with about 1 to $1^1/_2$ cups of their cooking water, and process until smooth.

3. Meanwhile, heat the oil in a medium pot over medium heat. Add the onion, garlic, sage, and rosemary. Cook, stirring, until the onion begins to color, 5 to 6 minutes. Add the cannellini beans and stir once or twice. Add the broth and bring to a gentle boil. Reduce the heat to low and simmer 40 to 50 minutes, or until the beans are tender. Season with salt and pepper.

4. Add the puréed beans to the pot with the white beans and bring to a gentle boil over low heat. Simmer 5 to 6 minutes. Stir in the parsley, taste, adjust the seasoning, and serve. Drizzle a few drops of olive oil over each serving. *Makes 4 to 6 servings.*

Prepare ahead

Through step 4, several hours to a day ahead. Cover and refrigerate.
Reheat the soup gently at the time of serving. Place in soup bowls, and drizzle with olive oil.

All good cooks, like all great artists, must have an audience worth cooking for.
—André Simon

TORTILLA SOUP WITH CHILES AND JACK CHEESE

6 corn tortillas

3/4 cup corn oil

2 medium onions, diced

3 garlic cloves, minced

1 jalapeño pepper, cored, seeded and minced

Pinch of chili pepper flakes

2 tablespoons chopped fresh cilantro or parsley

1 teaspoon ground cumin

6 cups chicken broth

1 cup canned plum tomatoes with their juice, put through a food mill to remove the seeds

Salt

4 ounces jack cheese, grated

1. Break 4 of the tortillas into very small pieces with your hands, or chop them roughly with a knife. Heat 4 tablespoons of the oil in a medium saucepan over medium heat. Add broken tortillas, onion, garlic, jalapeño, pepper flakes, and cilantro. Cook, stirring constantly, 2 to 3 minutes. Add cumin, stir once or twice, then add chicken broth and tomatoes, and season with salt. Bring soup to a boil, then reduce the heat to low. Simmer, uncovered, 30 to 40 minutes.

2. Heat remaining oil in a medium skillet over medium-high heat. Quarter remaining 2 tortillas. When the oil is very hot, fry the pieces in single layers until golden on both sides, about 1 minute. Transfer to paper towels to drain.

3. Preheat the broiler. Ladle the soup into ovenproof bowls. Place one piece of fried tortilla on top of each serving and sprinkle with grated cheese. Place bowls under the broiler until the cheese is melted and has a light golden color, 1 to 2 minutes. Serve piping hot. *Makes 6 to 8 servings.*

Prepare ahead
Through step 2, several hours ahead.
Ten minutes before you are ready to serve, reheat the soup gently.
Preheat the broiler, and complete step 3.

PASTA SALAD WITH SHRIMP, BROCCOLI, AND SUN-DRIED TOMATOES

The cooking time for pasta varies greatly from brand to brand. Select an Italian brand of pasta and check the cooking time given on the box. Taste the pasta several times to determine its doneness. To serve this salad as an entrée, just double the amount of shrimp. It will serve four generously.

1 bunch broccoli (1^1/$_2$ to 2 pounds)

Salt

^{1}/$_3$ cup olive oil

2 to 3 garlic cloves, minced

^{1}/$_4$ cup diced sun-dried tomatoes (packed in oil)

4 anchovy fillets, chopped

1 pound medium shrimp, peeled and deveined

1 pound pasta, such as penne or shells

2 to 3 tablespoons red wine vinegar

2 to 3 tablespoons additional olive oil

2 tablespoons chopped fresh parsley, or 8 to 10 fresh basil leaves shredded

Freshly ground pepper

1. Wash the broccoli. Remove and discard the bottom third of the tough stalks. Separate florets from the stalks. Peel remaining stalks and slice them into rounds. Bring a medium saucepan of salted water to a boil over medium heat. Add florets and sliced stalks, and cook until they are tender but still a bit firm, 3 to 4 minutes. Drain and rinse under cold running water. Pat dry with paper towels and place in a large bowl. Set aside.

2. Heat the oil in a large skillet over medium heat. Add the garlic, sun-dried tomatoes, and anchovies, and stir for less than one minute. Raise the heat, and add the shrimp. Cook, stirring, until shrimp are pink on both sides and cooked all the way through, about 4 minutes. Add the shrimp with all its sauce to the broccoli and mix well.

3. Bring a large pot of water to a boil over high heat. Add a pinch of salt and the pasta. Cook, uncovered, until pasta is tender but still a bit firm, 7 to 10 minutes. Drain pasta and rinse under cold running water. Shake the colander well to remove as much water as possible, then add the pasta to the bowl with the shrimp and broccoli.

◀ Pasta Salad with Shrimp, Broccoli, and Sun-Dried Tomatoes

4. In a small bowl, combine vinegar, additional olive oil, and parsley, and mix well. Season pasta with salt and several twists of pepper, and add the dressing. Mix thoroughly. Taste, adjust the seasoning, and serve. *Makes 6 servings.*

Prepare ahead

Through step 3, several hours ahead. Cover and refrigerate.
Dress the salad, step 4, just before serving.

Cooking is the soul of every pleasure at all times and to all ages. How many marriages have been the consequences of meeting at dinner, how much good fortune has been the result of a good supper, at what moment of our existence are we happier that at table? There hatred and animosity are lulled to sleep, and pleasure alone reigns.
—Anonymous

BABY ARTICHOKES AND POTATO SALAD

Artichokes have always been a favorite of the Mediterranean people. In Italy, where artichokes originated more than 2,000 years ago, they are extremely popular and are used in many appetizing preparations. For this salad, I chose baby artichokes because they are quick to clean and quick to cook and are just as delectable as their larger counterparts.

Baking potatoes are quite starchy and will absorb the oil very quickly. Do not skimp on the oil and seasoning or the salad will not have that wonderful "I can't stop eating it" quality. You can also prepare this salad with new potatoes.

2 pounds baking potatoes, peeled and cut into ¹/₄-inch round slices

2 pounds baby artichokes

Juice of 1 lemon

Salt

1 medium red onion, thinly sliced

2 garlic cloves, minced

¹/₂ cup extra-virgin olive oil

3 to 4 tablespoons red wine vinegar

Freshly ground pepper

1 tablespoon chopped fresh parsley

1. Place the potatoes in a medium saucepan and cover them generously with cold water. Bring the water to a boil over medium heat, and cook until tender, 10 to 15 minutes. Drain the potatoes, place in a salad bowl, and set aside to cool.

2. Remove the green leaves of the artichokes by snapping them off at the base. Stop when the leaves closer to the base are pale yellow and the tip of the artichokes are green. Slice off the green top. Cut the stem off at the base, and, with a small knife, trim off the remaining green part at the base. Place the artichokes in a bowl of cold water with the lemon juice to prevent discoloring.

3. Bring a medium saucepan of water to a boil over medium heat. Add 1 teaspoon of salt and the artichokes. Cook gently, 7 to 10 minutes, depending on size. Prick the bottom of one artichoke with a toothpick or a thin knife. If it goes in without resistance, the artichokes are done. Drain artichokes and cool under cold running water. Pat dry with paper towels, place in the bowl with the potatoes, and add the onion. (If the artichokes are small, leave them whole, if they are large, cut them in halves.)

4. In a small bowl mix the garlic with the olive oil, and pour over the potatoes. Sprinkle with the vinegar, and season generously with salt and pepper. Add the parsley, and mix well. Taste, adjust the seasoning, and serve. *Makes 4 to 6 servings.*

Prepare ahead

Through step 3, several hours ahead.
Step 4, dress the salad one half hour before or just before serving.

. . . a man hath no better thing under the sun, than to eat,
and to drink, and to be merry. . . .
—The Bible: Ecclesiastes 8:15

TOMATO, MOZZARELLA, AND GRILLED BREAD SALAD

2 large slices Italian or French bread, cut $1/2$-inch thick

1 large garlic clove, peeled and halved

4 large tomatoes, halved, seeded, and cut into $1/2$-inch cubes

2 tablespoons capers, rinsed

10 small, pitted green olives, quartered

$1/2$ small red onion minced

10 to 12 large fresh basil leaves, shredded, or 1 to 2 tablespoons chopped fresh parsley

6 ounces mozzarella, preferably fresh Italian mozzarella in water, cut into $1/2$-inch cubes

Salt and freshly ground pepper

$1/3$ to $1/2$ cup olive oil, preferably extra-virgin

2 to 3 tablespoons red wine vinegar

2 medium Belgian endive, leaves separated, washed, and dried

18 medium, unblemished, crisp, spinach leaves

1. Preheat the oven. Grill the bread in the oven or under the broiler until golden on both sides and rub with the cut garlic. When the bread is cool, cut it into $1/2$-inch pieces. Set aside until ready to use.

2. Place the bread, tomatoes, capers, olives, onion, basil, and mozzarella in a medium bowl. Season with salt and pepper and dress with olive oil and vinegar. Mix gently to combine.

3. Put the salad in a mound in the center of serving dishes. Alternate 3 endive leaves and 3 spinach leaves around each salad and serve. *Makes 6 servings.*

Prepare ahead

Do all the preparation for the salad, (grilling the bread, slicing the olives, dicing the tomatoes and mozzarella, etc.) several hours ahead of time.

Assemble and complete the salad, steps 2 and 3, just before serving.

SUZETTE SWORDFISH SALAD WITH ROASTED ONION AND TOMATOES

Suzette Gresham, a talented San Francisco chef, shared this lovely dish with me.

The method of poaching fish this way is the one used by Sicilian fishermen who, after catching tuna and swordfish off the coast of Sicily, cut the fish into fillets, then poach and preserve them in olive oil.

The oil of the marinade can be re-used in a variety of fish preparations, from pasta with fish, to fish stews and fish salads.

For the Fish

2 lemons, sliced

1 large onion, sliced

$1/2$ tablespoon salt

$1^1/2$ pounds swordfish steak, 1-inch thick

$2^1/2$ to 3 cups olive oil

To Complete the Dish

4 tablespoons olive oil

3 large onions with the skin on, cut into 1-inch thick wedges

Salt and freshly ground pepper

6 large plum tomatoes, halved lengthwise

A splash of good, strong red wine vinegar

1. *To poach the fish:* Fill a large saucepan halfway with water. Add lemon slices, onion, and salt, and bring to a boil over medium heat. Reduce the heat to low and simmer 10 to 15 minutes. Add the swordfish and immediately remove the saucepan from the heat. Leave the fish in the hot poaching liquid for 15 to 20 minutes or until it is cooked through.

2. Remove swordfish from the poaching liquid and pat dry with paper towels. (Do not worry if it breaks.) Place fish in a large bowl, completely cover it with olive oil, and cool to room temperature. Cover the bowl tightly with plastic wrap and refrigerate until ready to use.

3. *To roast the onions and tomatoes:* Preheat the oven to 400°F. Put two tablespoons of the olive oil in a baking pan and add onion wedges. Coat wedges with oil and season generously with salt and pepper. Bake until onions are golden brown and have a slightly caramelized look, 1 to $1^1/4$ hours.

◄ Suzette Swordfish Salad with Roasted Onion and Tomatoes

4. Meanwhile, put the remaining oil in the bottom of another baking pan and add tomatoes, cut side up. Brush tomatoes with a bit of additional oil and season with salt and pepper. Bake until tomatoes are soft, shriveled, and somewhat charred, 25 to 30 minutes.

5. Remove tomatoes and onions when they are done and cool to room temperature. Discard the skin of the onions and slice the wedges into thin strips. Place them in a bowl and sprinkle lightly with vinegar.

6. Lift the swordfish out of the oil and break into 1- to 2-inch pieces. Arrange the pieces in the center of the plates and top fish with some onions. Arrange tomatoes cut side down around the fish and serve. *Makes 6 servings.*

Prepare ahead

Through step 2, a day or two ahead. Bring the fish back to room temperature for a couple of hours before serving.

Steps 3, 4, and 5 can be done in the morning. Keep vegetables tightly covered at room temperature.

Complete step 6 just before serving.

Cooking is like love . . . it should be entered into with abandon, or not at all.
—Harriet van Horne

ORANGE, FENNEL, AND RADICCHIO SALAD

6 large oranges

$^1/_2$ medium fennel bulb, diced, tough outer leaves and root end removed (see page 30)

2 tablespoons chopped fennel green feathery tops

1 cup diced radicchio, loosely packed

4 long green onions, sliced

Salt

$^1/_3$ cup olive oil, preferably extra-virgin

2 to 3 tablespoons lemon juice

1. Peel the oranges with a sharp knife, taking care to remove all the white pith. Slice the oranges into $^1/_4$-inch thick rounds and remove the seeds. Cut each slice into quarters and place in a large salad bowl. Chill oranges for about one hour.

2. Just before serving, place fennel, fennel tops, radicchio, and onion in the bowl with the oranges. Season with salt and dress with the oil and the lemon juice. Toss lightly, taste, adjust the seasoning, and serve. *Makes 4 to 6 servings.*

Prepare ahead
Through step 1, a few hours ahead.
Complete step 2, just before serving.

BRUSCHETTA WITH FRESH TOMATOES AND GRILLED EGGPLANT

Do not assemble the tomato mixture too far ahead or the tomatoes will release their juice, which will make the bread soggy. When I prepare this dish, I keep the tomatoes in a strainer over a bowl, then assemble all the ingredients 10 minutes or so before I am ready to top the bread and bake it.

8 slices of good crusty Italian or French bread, cut into ¹/₂-inch thick slices

2 to 3 garlic cloves, peeled and halved

1 medium Japanese eggplant, cut into ¹/₄-inch thick rounds

6 plum tomatoes (about 1 pound), seeded and diced

2 tablespoons capers, rinsed

8 pitted black olives, quartered

6 to 8 fresh basil leaves, shredded, or 1 tablespoon chopped fresh parsley

2 tablespoons olive oil

Salt and freshly ground black pepper

4 ounces mozzarella, diced or grated

1. Preheat broiler. Put the bread on a baking sheet and toast under the broiler or in the oven until lightly golden on both sides. Rub one side of the bread with garlic.

2. Put the eggplant slices on a broiler pan, brush lightly with olive oil, and broil until golden on both sides. Cut the slices into small pieces.

3. In a small bowl combine eggplant, tomatoes, capers, olives, basil or parsley, and olive oil. Season with salt and several generous twists of pepper.

4. Spoon the mixture over the bread and sprinkle with mozzarella. Put the baking sheet under the broiler or in a 400°F preheated oven until the cheese is melted, 2 to 3 minutes. Cool slightly and serve. *Makes 4 servings.*

Prepare ahead
Through step 2, several hours ahead.
Complete steps 3 and 4 just before serving.

EGGPLANT CAPONATA

Caponata is a quintessential Sicilian dish. All the complexity and simplicity of Sicilian food can be found in this dish, where humble, everyday ingredients are bound together in a sweet and sour compote. This version of caponata omits the classic puréed tomatoes in favor of diced, fresh tomatoes, and the cooking time is also reduced considerably. The result is a caponata with a fresher look and taste. Caponata, generally served as an appetizer, can be equally enticing when served as a side dish.

1 small eggplant with skin on, diced into $1/2$-inch cubes

Salt

$1/2$ cup olive oil

1 small onion, diced

1 garlic clove, minced

1 large firm ripe tomato, seeded and diced

$1/3$ cup sugar

$1/3$ cup red wine vinegar

$1/4$ cup pine nuts

$1/4$ cup golden raisins, soaked in 1 cup water for 20 minutes, then drained

Italian bread

1. Put the eggplant cubes in a colander, sprinkle liberally with salt, and let stand for 1 hour. (The salt will draw out the eggplant's bitter juices.) Rinse eggplant quickly under cold running water and pat dry thoroughly with a kitchen towel.

2. Heat the oil in a large skillet over medium-high heat. Add the eggplant without crowding the skillet and cook the cubes to a golden color. (You might have to cook eggplant in a couple of batches.) Remove with a slotted spoon, place on paper towels, pat dry, and place into a medium bowl.

3. Return skillet to medium heat and add the onion. (If necessary, add a bit of additional oil.) Cook, stirring, until onion is lightly golden, 4 to 5 minutes. With a slotted spoon, transfer onion to eggplant. Add garlic and tomato to the skillet, stir a few times, then add to eggplant.

4. Raise the heat under the skillet and add the sugar, vinegar, pine nuts, and raisins. Season lightly with salt. Stir with a wooden spoon until sauce has a medium-thick, glazy consistency. Add to vegetables and mix gently, but thoroughly. Set aside, and cool to room temperature. Arrange caponata in a small mound on a serving dish and serve with grilled or toasted Italian bread. *Makes 4 to 6 servings as an appetizer or side dish.*

Prepare ahead
Completely through step 4 several hours ahead.

A good meal soothes the soul as it regenerates the body.
—Fredrick W. Hackwood

LOVING DINNERS FOR FRIENDS

Entrées

Spicy Scallops and Rice Salad

Swordfish Bundles Stuffed with Shrimp

Tuna Steaks with Sweet and Sour Sauce

Chicken Stew with Vinegar, Tomatoes, and Green Olives

Roasted Chicken Breasts with Roasted Onions, Potatoes, and
Balsamic Vinegar

Chicken Breasts Stuffed with Mushrooms and Prosciutto in
Marsala Wine Sauce

Roasted Turkey Breast with Vegetables

Stuffed Turkey Breast Braised in Milk

Pork Roast with Prunes and Madeira Wine

Steak Salad with Peppercorns, Coriander, and Ginger

Pot Roast with Onions and White Beans

Oven-Braised Veal Shanks with Artichokes

Veal Stew with Marsala Wine and Mixed Mushrooms

SPICY SCALLOPS AND RICE SALAD

For this dish, try to select the smallest scallops possible. If scallops are quite large, slice them in half horizontally. In this case, you may need to reduce the cooking time. Scallops are cooked when they are chalky white all the way through. Have the oil in the skillet very hot and do not crowd the skillet, allowing the scallops' juices to quickly evaporate. The scallops will brown in no time at all.

Arborio rice is a short-grain, plump rice that is used extensively in Italian cooking for risotto preparations and rice salads.

$1^1/_2$ **cups Italian Arborio rice, or short grain California pearl rice**

$1/_2$ **cup olive oil**

$1^1/_2$ **pounds bay or sea scallops**

2 garlic cloves, minced

Chili pepper flakes to taste

2 tablespoons capers, rinsed

$1/_2$ **small red onion, thinly sliced**

2 tablespoons chopped fresh parsley

4 large firm ripe tomatoes, seeded and diced

Juice of 2 lemons

Salt

1. Bring a medium saucepan of salted water to a boil over high heat. Add the rice and reduce the heat to medium. Cook until rice is tender but still a bit firm to the bite, 10 to 12 minutes. Drain rice and rinse it under cold running water to stop the cooking. Drain well and place in a large bowl until ready to use.

2. Heat 2 to 3 tablespoons of the oil in a large skillet over high heat. Add the scallops. Cook, stirring, until scallops are slightly golden and are cooked all the way through, about 4 minutes. Remove skillet from heat, add garlic and pepper flakes, and stir once or twice. Transfer the contents of the skillet to a bowl and cool to room temperature.

3. Add scallops and all of the juices to the rice. Add capers, onion, parsley, and diced tomatoes. Season with salt. Dress salad with remaining oil and lemon juice and mix well. Taste, adjust the seasoning, and serve. *Makes 4 to 6 servings.*

Prepare ahead
Through step 2, several hours ahead. Cover and refrigerate.
Complete step 3 just before serving.

SWORDFISH BUNDLES STUFFED WITH SHRIMP

$1/2$ pound small, precooked baby shrimp

2 to 3 slices white bread, crust removed, soaked in 2 cups low-fat milk for 10 minutes

$1/3$ cup freshly grated Parmigiano-Reggiano

2 tablespoons chopped fresh parsley

2 garlic cloves, minced

Salt and freshly ground pepper

2 large eggs, lightly beaten in a small bowl

12 swordfish steaks, sliced $1/8$-inch thick, about 4 ounces each, pounded thin

$1/3$ cup olive oil, mixed with 2 tablespoons red wine vinegar

$1/3$ cup dry, unseasoned bread crumbs, mixed with 1 tablespoon olive oil and 1 tablespoon chopped parsley

1. Chop the shrimp very fine by hand or with a food processor and place into a bowl. (If using a food processor, make sure not to chop them into a paste.)

2. Squeeze all of the milk from the bread and add bread to the shrimp. Add the Parmigiano, parsley, and garlic, and season with salt and several twists of pepper. Mix everything together and correct the seasoning.

3. Place the swordfish steaks on a work surface. Spread some shrimp mixture in the center of each steak and roll it into bundles. Secure each bundle with a few toothpicks.

4. Preheat the barbecue or broiler. Brush the bundles with the olive oil and vinegar, and sprinkle lightly with the bread crumb mixture. Place bundles over the hot rack of the barbecue or in the broiler pan. (Broil 2 to 3 inches from the heat source.) Cook until bundles are golden brown on all sides, 6 to 8 minutes. Turn them gently a few times and baste with the oil and vinegar. Serve hot. *Makes 6 servings.*

Prepare ahead

Through step 3, several hours ahead, cover and refrigerate.
Complete step 4 just before serving.

TUNA STEAKS WITH SWEET AND SOUR SAUCE

$^1/_3$ cup olive oil

4 tuna or swordfish steaks,
   1-inch thick (about 2 pounds)

Salt and freshly ground pepper

1 small yellow onion, minced

2 garlic cloves, minced

2 tablespoons sugar mixed with
   $^1/_3$ cup red wine vinegar

$^1/_3$ cup golden raisins, softened
   in lukewarm water and
   drained

1 to 2 tablespoons capers,
   drained and rinsed

2 cups canned plum tomatoes
   with their juice, put through a
   food mill to remove the seeds

1. Heat the oil in a large skillet over medium heat. Add the steaks and cook until they are lightly golden on both sides, 3 to 4 minutes. Season steaks with salt and pepper and transfer them to paper towels.

2. Add onion and garlic to the skillet and cook over medium-low heat, stirring, until onion is lightly golden, 4 to 5 minutes. Add the sugar/vinegar mixture, raisins, and capers. Cook, stirring, until vinegar is completely reduced, 1 to 2 minutes. Add the tomatoes and season with salt and pepper.

3. Return the tuna steaks to the skillet and bring the sauce to a gentle simmer. Cover and simmer 4 to 5 minutes. Taste, adjust the seasoning and serve. *Makes 4 servings.*

Prepare ahead
Through step 3, 1 to 2 hours ahead. Cover and refrigerate.
Reheat gently before serving.

CHICKEN STEW WITH VINEGAR, TOMATOES, AND GREEN OLIVES

1/4 cup extra-virgin olive oil

Salt and freshly ground pepper

1 plump stewing chicken (about 4 pounds), cut into 8 pieces

3 garlic cloves, minced

6 to 7 fresh sage leaves, minced, or 1 teaspoon crumbled dry sage

Pinch of chili pepper flakes (optional)

2 tablespoons chopped fresh rosemary, or 1 teaspoon dried rosemary, crushed

1/2 cup red wine vinegar

1/2 cup chicken broth

2 cups canned plum tomatoes with their juice, put through a food mill to remove the seeds

1/3 cup pitted green olives, quartered

1 tablespoon chopped fresh parsley

1. Heat the oil in a large skillet over medium-high heat. Season the chicken with salt and pepper. When the oil is hot, add the chicken to the skillet, skin side down, without crowding. (If necessary, the chicken can be browned in two batches.) Cook until chicken pieces are golden on all sides, 8 to 10 minutes. Transfer chicken to a platter.

2. Discard half of the fat in the skillet and place skillet back on the heat. Add garlic, sage, pepper flakes (if using), and rosemary, and stir quickly once or twice. (Remember that the skillet is very hot and garlic will brown in no time at all). Add vinegar and stir to pick up the bits and pieces attached to the bottom of the skillet. Cook until vinegar is reduced roughly by half. Add broth, tomatoes, and olives, and bring to a boil. Return chicken to the skillet and reduce the heat to low. Cover skillet, with the lid slightly askew, and simmer 25 to 30 minutes or until chicken is done all the way through and sauce has a medium-thick consistency. Baste and turn chicken a few times during cooking.

3. Place chicken on serving dishes. Stir parsley into the sauce. Season lightly with salt, taste, and adjust the seasoning. Spoon sauce over the chicken. *Makes 4 servings.*

Prepare ahead
Through step 2, several hours ahead. Cover and refrigerate.
Reheat the chicken and complete step 3 just before serving.

ROASTED CHICKEN BREASTS WITH ROASTED ONIONS, POTATOES, AND BALSAMIC VINEGAR

Since it takes approximately one hour to properly cook and brown the onions to a golden color, we shorten the cooking time by prebaking them. The onions will then finish cooking at the last moment with the chicken and the potatoes.

$^1/_2$ **cup olive oil**

$^1/_3$ **cup balsamic vinegar**

2 large onions, peeled, with their root ends on, and quartered

1 pound small red new potatoes, scrubbed and halved

Salt and freshly ground pepper

4 whole chicken breasts (about 1 pound each), with bone and skin, split

4 whole garlic cloves, peeled

1. Preheat the oven to 400°F. Mix 3 tablespoons of the oil and 2 tablespoons of the vinegar in a small baking dish and add the onions. Toss the onions gently to coat with the oil and vinegar. Bake until the onions are lightly golden, 20 to 25 minutes. Stir once or twice during cooking. Remove from the oven and set aside until ready to use.

2. Meanwhile, season the chicken with salt and pepper on both sides. Heat 2 tablespoons of the remaining oil in a large ovenproof skillet over medium-high heat. When the oil is very hot, add the chicken, skin side down, and cook until lightly golden, 2 to 3 minutes. Turn the chicken, and brown the other side, 2 to 3 minutes. Add reserved onions, potatoes, garlic, remaining olive oil and vinegar to the skillet, and mix well.

3. Place the skillet in the 400°F oven. Bake 20 to 25 minutes, or until chicken is cooked all the way through and the potatoes and onions are golden brown and glazed. Stir potatoes and onions a few times during cooking and baste chicken with pan juices or with a bit of additional vinegar. Serve hot. *Makes 4 servings.*

Prepare ahead
Through step 1, several hours or a day ahead. Cover and refrigerate.
Steps 2 and 3, one half hour ahead. Reheat just before serving.

CHICKEN BREASTS STUFFED WITH MUSHROOMS AND PROSCIUTTO IN MARSALA WINE SAUCE

These chicken bundles are pan roasted in the Italian manner. This cooking method produces a delicate, tender chicken with minimal effort. Make sure to turn chicken a few times during cooking and to stir the pan juices occasionally. By partially covering the skillet with a lid, the liquid reduces slowly, leaving just enough sauce in the pan to give moisture and taste to the chicken. The high sugar content in the marsala wine will give the chicken a beautiful, golden color and the sauce a rich, glazy consistency. Madeira wine can be substituted for marsala.

Other types of mushrooms can also be used. If available, try some shiitakes and chanterelles to enhance the taste of this dish.

For the Mushrooms

1 ounce dry porcini mushrooms soaked in 2 cups lukewarm water for 20 minutes

3 to 4 tablespoons olive oil

1/4 pound white cultivated mushrooms, wiped clean with a damp cloth and finely minced

1 small garlic clove, minced

1 tablespoon chopped fresh parsley

1/4 cup marsala wine

2 to 3 tablespoons freshly grated Parmigiano-Reggiano

Salt and freshly ground pepper

For the Chicken

4 whole chicken breasts (about 1 pound each), boned and split, with skin on, flattened

8 thin slices of prosciutto (about 1/4 pound) or thinly sliced baked or smoked ham

1/4 cup olive oil

1 cup marsala wine

1 tablespoon unsalted butter

1. *Prepare the mushrooms:* Drain the porcini mushrooms and reserve the soaking water. Rinse the porcini thoroughly under cold running water to remove any sandy deposits, then chop them fine. Strain the reserved soaking water through a few layers of paper towels until clear. Set aside until ready to use.

2. Heat the oil in a medium skillet over high heat. When the oil is very hot, add the white mushrooms and the porcini and cook, stirring, until they begin to color, 1 to 2 minutes. Add the garlic and parsley, and stir once or twice. Add the wine and cook, always stirring, until wine is all reduced, 1 to 2 minutes. Transfer mushrooms to a bowl and cool to room temperature. Stir Parmigiano into cooled mushrooms and season lightly with salt and pepper. Set aside until ready to use.

3. *Prepare the chicken:* Place the chicken on a work surface. Top each half breast with one slice of prosciutto and spread some mushrooms over the prosciutto leaving a free border all around the chicken. Fold the two sides of the chicken to barely cover the filling, then roll the chicken into bundles. Secure each breast with a couple of wooden picks, or tie with strings so that the filling will not fall out while cooking.

4. Heat the oil in a large skillet over medium-high heat. Season breasts with salt and pepper, and add them to the skillet. Cook until lightly golden on all sides, 6 to 8 minutes. Discard all but 1 tablespoon of fat in the skillet and add $^1/_2$ cup of the wine. Cook, stirring, until wine is roughly reduced by half. Cover the skillet with lid slightly askew, and lower the heat to low. Simmer chicken 15 to 20 minutes, turning the breasts and stirring occasionally, until chicken is cooked all the way through. Add a bit of reserved porcini mushroom water if liquid in the skillet reduces too much. Remove wooden picks, or string, from chicken and place bundles on serving dishes. Keep warm in a low-heated oven while you finish the sauce.

5. Put skillet back on very high heat. When very hot, add remaining wine, butter, and $^1/_4$ cup of reserved porcini soaking water. Cook, stirring constantly, until sauce has a medium-thick consistency and a glazed golden color, about 1 minute. Taste and adjust the seasoning. Spoon sauce over chicken and serve at once. *Makes 4 servings.*

Prepare ahead
Through step 4, one hour or so ahead. Cover and refrigerate instead of placing in oven. Reheat chicken and complete step 5 just before serving.

ROASTED TURKEY BREAST
WITH VEGETABLES

In this preparation the roast is browned on the stove, the vegetables are added to the pot, and as guests arrive, the roast is put in the oven to finish cooking. Keep in mind that the cooking time of a roast depends more on its thickness than its weight. It is obvious that a long, thin, four-pound roast will cook much faster than a thick, round roast of the same weight.

3$^1/_2$ to 4 pounds boneless turkey breast, tied into a roast

1 sprig finely chopped fresh rosemary, or 1 tablespoon dried rosemary, crushed

Salt and freshly ground pepper

$^1/_3$ to $^1/_2$ cup olive oil

1 cup dry white wine

3 carrots, scraped and cut into thick rounds

3 baking potatoes, peeled and cut into medium chunks

3 red bell peppers, seeded and cut into 1-inch strips

1 large yellow onion, peeled and quartered

4 garlic cloves, peeled

1. Preheat the oven to 375°F. Rub the roast all over with the chopped rosemary and season with salt and pepper.

2. Heat the oil in a large ovenproof casserole over medium-high heat. When the oil is very hot, add the roast and brown on all sides, 8 to 10 minutes. (If the oil turns too dark during the browning of the meat, discard it, and add fresh oil.)

3. Raise the heat to high and add the wine. Cook and stir, turning the turkey and scraping the bottom of the casserole with a wooden spoon, until the wine is almost all reduced, 5 to 6 minutes. Add all the vegetables and the garlic, and mix them well, making sure they are well coated with the oil and the pan juices.

4. Place roast in the oven and bake about 1 hour, or until it reads 160°F on a meat thermometer. Baste the roast several times during cooking with pan juices or with a bit of additional wine. Transfer roast to a cutting board and let it rest 5 to 10 minutes.

5. Push the vegetables to one side of the casserole and spoon off about half of the fat in the pan. Keep the vegetables warm over low heat while you slice the meat. Serve roast with some of the roasted vegetables and pan juices. (The vegetables will become soft and golden and will probably stick a bit to the bottom of the pot. This is all right because they will taste even better.) *Makes 6 servings.*

Prepare ahead
Through step 4, half hour or so ahead.
Complete step 5 just before serving.

The No. 1 rule to being a good host is to stay out of the
kitchen as much as possible.
—Margaret Visser

STUFFED TURKEY BREAST BRAISED IN MILK

Pork braised in milk is a classic dish of my region of Emilia-Romagna. There, the pork is browned in oil and butter, and finished cooking slowly in milk. This cooking method gives the meat a delicate taste and tender consistency. One day while I was browning a stuffed turkey roast over the stove, I switched gears and decided to simmer the meat in milk instead of roasting it in the oven. I could not have been happier with the result!

3¹/₂ to 4 pounds boneless turkey breast, butterflied and pounded evenly thin

Salt and freshly ground pepper

¹/₄ pound thinly sliced prosciutto, or baked ham

¹/₄ to ¹/₃ cup olive oil

1 tablespoon unsalted butter

4 cups milk

1 cup chicken broth

¹/₂ cup heavy cream

¹/₄ cup freshly grated Parmigiano-Reggiano

1 tablespoon chopped fresh parsley

1. Place turkey breast on a work surface, season the inner side with salt and pepper, and cover with the prosciutto or ham slices. Roll the meat tightly and tie securely with string.

2. Heat the oil over medium-high heat in a pan that fits the roast snugly. As soon as the oil is hot, season the roast lightly with salt and add it to the pan. Cook until turkey is lightly golden on all sides, 8 to 10 minutes.

3. Discard about half of the fat in the pan. Add the butter and the milk, and bring the milk to a boil. Reduce the heat to low and cover the pan with the lid slightly askew. Cook 1 to 1^1/$_4$ hours or until the turkey breast reads 160°F on a meat thermometer. Baste and turn the meat a few times during cooking. At the end of the cooking time, there should be approximately 1 to 1^1/$_2$ cups of milky residue still left in the pan.

4. Remove the lid and raise the heat to high. Cook, stirring until the milk is almost all evaporated and only brown clusters of thickened sauce are left in the pan. Transfer turkey roast to a wooden board while you finish the sauce. (At this point, the internal temperature of the meat should read 165°F on a meat thermometer.)

5. Tilt the pan and remove as much fat as possible. Put the pan back on high heat, add the broth, and bring to a quick boil. Cook and stir to pick up all the bits and pieces attached to the bottom of the pan. Put the sauce in the bowl of a food processor fitted with the metal blade. Add the cream and Parmigiano, and process until smooth. Return sauce to the saucepan. Add parsley, taste, and adjust the seasoning. Bring sauce to a gentle boil, stir once or twice, then return roast to the pot. Turn off the heat and set aside.

6. Just before serving, slice the meat and reheat the sauce gently over low heat. Serve roast with a few tablespoons of sauce. *Makes 6 servings.*

Prepare ahead
Through step 5, a half hour or so ahead.
Complete step 6 just before serving.

> *Properly considered, the quality of the dinner is twice blest; it blesses him that gives and him that takes; a dinner with friendliness is the best of all satisfactory meetings.*
> —*Punch* magazine

PORK ROAST WITH PRUNES AND MADEIRA WINE

Because prunes will absorb a considerable amount of sauce, you might need to add more liquid at the time of reheating.

3 pounds boneless center cut, pork loin roast, securely tied

Salt and freshly ground pepper

$^1/_4$ cup olive oil

1 cup Madeira or marsala wine

1 tablespoon unsalted butter

$^1/_2$ cup chicken broth

$^1/_4$ cup heavy cream

6 ounces pitted prunes, diced

1. Season the pork loin with salt and pepper. Heat the oil in a large, heavy casserole over medium-high heat. When oil is very hot, add the meat and brown on all sides, 8 to 10 minutes.

2. Discard half of the fat in the casserole and return it to high heat. Add $^1/_2$ cup of the wine and stir quickly with a wooden spoon, turning the meat once or twice. Partially cover casserole and reduce the heat to low. Simmer the meat slowly, turning and basting it several times during cooking, until pork is cooked all the way through, approximately $1^1/_2$ hours, or until it reads 155°F on a meat thermometer. If sauce reduces too much, add a splash of broth or wine. Transfer roast to a cutting board while you finish the sauce.

3. Spoon off as much fat as possible from pan juices. Raise the heat to high. When casserole is very hot, add the remaining wine, butter, broth, cream, and prunes. Cook, stirring, to pick up the bits and pieces on the bottom of the casserole until sauce has a medium-thick consistency, 1 to 2 minutes. Taste and adjust the seasoning. Put roast back in the casserole, cover, and let stand on top of the stove with no heat until ready to use.

4. Just before serving, slice the meat and arrange on serving dishes. If necessary, reheat the sauce gently and spoon over the meat. Serve at once. *Makes 6 servings.*

Prepare ahead
Through step 3, half hour ahead.
Complete step 4 just before serving.

STEAK SALAD WITH PEPPERCORNS, CORIANDER, AND GINGER

Black peppercorns and dry coriander seeds can be found in the spice section of supermarkets. Fresh ginger can be found in most supermarkets or in Oriental markets. To crush peppercorns and coriander, put them between two separate pieces of plastic wrap or parchment paper and press back and forth with a rolling pin, or pound them with a meat mallet.

For the Steak

2 pounds New York or rib eye steak, 1-inch thick	2 tablespoons dry coriander seeds, crushed
2 teaspoons sesame oil	2 tablespoons grated fresh ginger
2 tablespoons black peppercorns, crushed	3 to 4 tablespoons olive oil

For the Salad

1/2 pound snow peas	1/4 pound bean sprouts
1 small red onion, thinly sliced	

For the Dressing

2 teaspoons sesame oil	1 teaspoon soy sauce
2 tablespoons olive oil	Salt
1 tablespoon rice vinegar	

1. Prepare the steak: Preheat oven to 400°F. Brush the steaks with sesame oil. In a small bowl, combine peppercorns, coriander, and ginger. Spread mixture on steaks, pressing it into the meat.

2. Heat olive oil in a large ovenproof skillet over medium heat. Add the steaks and cook until golden brown on both sides, 3 to 4 minutes. Discard half of the fat and place skillet in the oven. Roast 4 to 5 minutes for medium rare and 6 to 7 minutes for medium. Transfer steaks to a cutting board and let stand for 10 minutes. Cut them diagonally into 1/4-inch thick slices.

◀ Steak Salad with Peppercorns, Coriander, and Ginger

3. *Prepare the salad and dressing:* In a large bowl, combine snow peas, onion, and bean sprouts. Stir together all the dressing ingredients in a small bowl. Pour all but one teaspoon of dressing over the salad and mix well. Taste and adjust the seasoning. Arrange salad in small mounds in the center of serving plates and place slices of beef around the salad. Drizzle remaining dressing over the steak and serve. *Makes 4 servings.*

Prepare ahead

Through step 2, a few hours ahead. In this case, keep steaks tightly wrapped in the refrigerator and bring to room temperature for 20 to 30 minutes before serving.
Complete step 3 just before serving.

We only eat to live when we don't understand how to live to eat.
—George Ellwanger

POT ROAST WITH ONIONS AND WHITE BEANS

A pot roast should simmer for several hours very slowly and it should be basted several times during cooking. Fast cooking will make the roast tough. This roast has a delicious sweet taste imparted by the prolonged cooking of the onions. The addition of the beans adds body and a wholesome taste to the dish.

1 cup dried white kidney beans, soaked overnight in cold water to cover

3 tablespoons olive oil

1 tablespoon unsalted butter

3 to 3$^{1}/_{2}$ pounds beef, bottom round or chuck

Salt and freshly ground pepper

$^{1}/_{2}$ cup all-purpose flour

3 large yellow onions (2 to 2$^{1}/_{2}$ pounds), thinly sliced

2 cups dry red wine, such as a pinot or chianti

1 cup canned tomatoes with their juice, put through a food mill to remove the seeds

1 cup beef broth

2 tablespoons chopped, fresh parsley

1. Discard any beans that come to the surface of the water. Drain and rinse the beans under cold running water and place in a medium saucepan. Cover beans with cold water 2 inches above the level of the beans and bring to a gentle boil, uncovered, over medium heat. Cook until beans are tender, 30 to 40 minutes. Stir a few times during cooking. Drain beans and set aside until ready to use.

2. Preheat the oven to 350°F. Heat the oil and butter in a large casserole over medium-high heat. When the butter foams, season meat with salt and pepper, sprinkle with flour, and add to the casserole. Cook meat until golden brown on all sides, 6 to 8 minutes. Transfer meat to a platter. (If the fat in the pot turns too dark during the browning of the meat, replace it with fresh oil and butter.) Reduce the heat to medium and add the onions. Cook, stirring, until onions are lightly golden, 5 to 6 minutes.

3. Return meat to casserole and raise the heat to high. Add the wine. Cook and stir for 2 to 3 minutes to reduce the wine a bit. Add the tomatoes and broth, and season with salt and several twists of pepper. As soon as the liquid comes to a boil, cover the casserole loosely with aluminum foil, and place in the oven. Bake 3 to 3¹/₂ hours, stirring and basting the meat every half hour or so. If the liquid in the pan reduces too much, add a bit more broth, wine, or tomatoes. Add the beans and mix well into the sauce. Cook 10 to 15 minutes longer. At this point, the meat should be quite tender and the sauce should have a thick consistency.

4. Place meat on a cutting board and let it rest 5 to 10 minutes. Taste the sauce and adjust the seasoning. If sauce is too thin, place it on high heat, and cook, stirring, until it is further reduced and has a medium-thick consistency. Stir in parsley.

5. Slice meat, place on serving dishes, and top with the sauce. Serve hot. *Makes 6 servings.*

Prepare ahead

Through step 4, several hours to a day ahead. Chill meat, then slice it, and place in the pot covered with its sauce. Keep it tightly covered in the refrigerator. Before serving, bring meat to room temperature, then reheat gently over moderate heat.

TIP: The best cuts of meat to use for pot roasts are the bottom round or the chuck. The bottom round is a fairly lean, solid piece of meat. The chuck, which generally comes tied up in a roast, has considerably more fat.

OVEN-BRAISED VEAL SHANKS
WITH ARTICHOKES

Cook the veal very slowly, just like a stew. Fast cooking will make the veal tough. If the sauce in the pot is too thin, cook it down over high heat, stirring constantly, until it reaches a medium-thick consistency. If the sauce has reduced too much, add a bit more broth to the pot and cook it until it is bound together with the other pan juices.

1 pound baby artichokes, cleaned, cooked, and halved (see page 91)	**1 tablespoon unsalted butter**
	1 medium onion, thinly sliced
8 veal shanks, 1½-inch thick, preferably cut from the veal hind shanks	**1 cup dry white wine**
	2½ cups chicken broth
Salt and freshly ground pepper	**2 tablespoons chopped fresh parsley**
1 cup all-purpose flour spread over a sheet of aluminum foil	**1 garlic clove, finely minced**
	Grated peel of 1 lemon
4 tablespoons olive oil	

1. Prepare the baby artichokes as instructed on page 91, and set aside until ready to use.

2. Preheat the oven to 350°F. Season the veal shanks with salt and pepper, and dredge them with flour. Shake off any excess flour. Heat the oil in a large, heavy, ovenproof pot over medium-high heat. When the oil is hot, add the veal and cook until golden on both sides, 6 to 7 minutes. Transfer meat to a dish.

3. Discard half of the fat and place the pot back on medium heat. Add the butter. As soon as the butter begins to foam, add the onion. Cook, stirring, until onion is lightly golden, 5 to 6 minutes. Add the wine and cook until it is roughly reduced by half. Add the broth, bring to a boil, then turn off the heat. Return shanks to the pot, cover it tightly with a lid, and place in the preheated oven. Bake 1½ hours, basting the meat several times during cooking. Add a bit more broth if liquid in the pan reduces too much.

4. Add artichokes to the pot and mix well with the sauce. Cover the pot and bake 10 to 15 minutes longer. (At this point, the meat should be quite tender, and will begin to fall away from the bone.)

5. Transfer shanks to a large warm serving dish. Put the pot on high heat and quickly stir in the parsley, garlic, and lemon peel. Stir the sauce a couple of times, taste it, adjust the seasoning, and pour it over the shanks. Serve at once. *Makes 4 servings.*

Prepare ahead

Through step 5, several hours to a day ahead. Keep veal shanks tightly covered in the refrigerator. When ready to serve, bring veal shanks to room temperature, reheat them gently, and serve.

TIP: Good veal shanks should come from milk-fed veal; if fresh veal shanks are not available at your local market, frozen veal shanks are perfectly acceptable. Select shanks that come from the hind part of the veal because they are meatier. Try to select shanks of the same size for even cooking.

VEAL STEW WITH MARSALA WINE AND MIXED MUSHROOMS

A stew calls for something starchy with it. Good crusty bread, boiled or steamed rice, soft or grilled polenta, or mashed potatoes can enrich this dish and make it even more appetizing.

If various types of mushrooms are not available or are too expensive, use white cultivated mushrooms. The stew will still be exceptionally good.

$^1/_2$ **cup olive oil**

3 pounds veal shoulder or stewing veal, cut into 2-inch pieces

1 cup all-purpose flour

1 cup dry marsala wine

1 medium onion, diced

2 garlic cloves, minced

2 tablespoons chopped fresh rosemary, or 1 teaspoon dried rosemary, crushed

8 to 10 fresh sage leaves, chopped, or 1 teaspoon crumbled dry sage

2 cups chicken broth

3 cups canned plum tomatoes with their juice put through a food mill or sieve to remove the seeds

Salt and freshly ground pepper

1 pound of assorted mushrooms, such as cultivated white, shiitake, brown, oyster or chanterelle, cleaned and thinly sliced

$^1/_4$ **cup additional olive oil for the mushrooms**

2 tablespoons chopped fresh parsley

1. Heat $^1/_3$ cup of the oil in a large heavy skillet over high heat. Place the veal in a large colander over a bowl, and sprinkle with flour. Shake the colander to distribute the flour evenly. Add the veal to the hot oil in batches and brown on all sides, 5 to 6 minutes. (Make sure not to crowd the skillet or the veal will not brown evenly.) Scoop up the browned veal with a slotted spoon, draining it against the side of the skillet, and transfer it to a platter. Once all the veal is browned, discard the fat in the skillet and return it to high heat. Add wine, and cook, stirring, to pick up all the flavorful bits and pieces attached to the bottom of the skillet. When the wine is reduced by half, pour it into a bowl and reserve until ready to use.

2. Put the skillet back on medium-high heat and add remaining oil. When the oil is hot, add onion, garlic, rosemary, and sage. Cook, stirring, until the onion is lightly golden, 4 to 5 minutes.

3. Return the veal to the skillet and raise the heat to high. Add the reserved wine, broth, and tomatoes. Season with salt and several twists of pepper and mix well. Bring the liquid to a boil. Cover the skillet, with the lid slightly askew, and reduce the heat to low. Simmer about 1 hour or until the meat is tender. At this point, the sauce should have a medium-thick consistency. Stir a few times during cooking.

4. While the stew is simmering, prepare the mushrooms. Heat $1/4$ cup oil in a large skillet over high heat. Add the mushrooms, making sure not to crowd the skillet (you might have to cook mushrooms in a few batches), and cook until lightly golden, 2 to 3 minutes. Drain the mushrooms on paper towels. Add mushrooms to the stew, during the last 10 minutes of cooking.

5. Just before serving, stir in parsley, taste, and adjust the seasoning. Serve hot. *Makes 6 servings.*

Prepare ahead
Through step 4, several hours to a day ahead.
Keep stew tightly covered in the refrigerator. When you are ready to serve, Step 5, bring stew to room temperature, then reheat it gently, and serve.

LOVING DINNERS FOR FRIENDS

Vegetables

Baby Artichokes with Sun-Dried Tomatoes and Garlic

Green Beans with Roasted Pine Nuts

Brussels Sprouts with Red Bell Peppers and Smoked Ham

Gratin of Cauliflower, Carrot, and Onion

Sautéed Mushroom Caps with Balsamic Vinegar

BABY ARTICHOKES WITH SUN-DRIED TOMATOES AND GARLIC

2 pounds baby artichokes,
cleaned, cooked, and halved
(see page 91)

2 tablespoons olive oil

2 garlic cloves, minced

1 tablespoon minced sun-dried
tomatoes (packed in oil)

1 tablespoon chopped fresh
parsley

Pinch of chili pepper flakes
(optional)

1 tablespoon dry, unseasoned
bread crumbs

$1/3$ cup dry white wine

2 tablespoons lemon juice

Salt

1. Prepare the baby artichokes as instructed on page 91, and set aside until ready to use.

2. Heat the oil in a medium skillet over medium heat. Add the garlic, sun-dried tomatoes, parsley, pepper flakes (if using), and bread crumbs, and stir a few times. Add the artichokes, wine, and lemon juice. Season with salt. Raise the heat and cook, stirring, just long enough to reduce the wine and to heat the artichokes through, 1 to 2 minutes. *Makes 4 servings.*

Prepare ahead
Through step 1, several hours or a day ahead. Cover and refrigerate.
Complete step 2 about one hour ahead.
Just before serving, reheat gently over low heat.

GREEN BEANS WITH ROASTED PINE NUTS

Pine nuts are the seeds of the stone pine, a tree native to the Mediterranean. Pine nuts can be eaten raw or roasted. They appear in many Italian dishes and are one of the essential ingredients of the traditional pesto sauce. To facilitate this simple dish, have the beans at room temperature and all your ingredients premeasured on a tray. In a minute or so the dish will be completed.

$1^1/_2$ **pounds green beans, the smallest available**

$^1/_3$ **cup pine nuts**

3 tablespoons olive oil

1 small garlic clove, minced

$^1/_4$ **cup fresh lemon juice**

1 tablespoon chopped fresh parsley, preferably flat leaf Italian parsley

Salt and freshly ground pepper

1. Snap off both ends of the green beans and wash them under cold running water. Bring a medium saucepan half full of salted water to a boil over medium high heat. Add the green beans and cook uncovered until tender but still a bit crunchy, 2 to 4 minutes depending on size. Drain and immediately plunge them in a large bowl of ice water to stop the cooking and to set the green color of the beans. Drain well.

2. Place the pine nuts in a small baking dish and toast, stirring often, until lightly golden, 3 to 5 minutes. Set aside.

3. Heat the oil in a medium skillet over medium heat. Add the garlic and stir once or twice. Add the green beans, lemon juice, pine nuts, and parsley, and season with salt and pepper. Raise the heat to high and cook, stirring, just long enough to heat the beans through, 1 to 2 minutes. *Makes 6 servings.*

Prepare ahead
Through step 2, several hours ahead.
Complete step 3 just before serving.

BRUSSELS SPROUTS WITH RED BELL PEPPERS AND SMOKED HAM

Brussels sprouts are miniature cabbages that are said to have originated in Brussels, Belgium. This hardy, winter vegetable is utterly delicious when paired with smoked ham and butter. The red bell peppers add a splash of contrasting color to the dish.

$1\frac{1}{2}$ **pounds Brussels sprouts, trimmed and washed**

3 to 4 tablespoons unsalted butter

2 small red bell peppers, cored, seeded, and cut into thin strips

$\frac{1}{3}$ **cup chicken broth or water**

$\frac{1}{4}$ **pound sliced smoked ham or prosciutto, cut into thin strips**

Salt and freshly ground pepper

1. Bring a medium saucepan half full of salted water to a boil over medium-high heat. Add the Brussels sprouts and lower the heat to medium. Cook, uncovered, until the sprouts are tender but still a bit firm to the bite, 6 to 10 minutes depending on size. Drain and immediately plunge them in a large bowl of ice water to stop the cooking and set in the green color of the sprouts.

2. Heat the butter in a medium skillet over medium heat. When the butter begins to foam, add the red bell peppers and the broth. Cook, stirring, until broth is completely reduced, 1 to 2 minutes.

3. Add the ham and Brussels sprouts, and season with salt and pepper. Stir for a few minutes until sprouts are heated all the way through and are coated with the butter. Serve at once. *Makes 4 to 6 servings.*

Prepare ahead
Through step 1, several hours ahead.
Complete steps 2 and 3 just before serving.

GRATIN OF CAULIFLOWER, CARROT, AND ONION

Do not skimp with the nutmeg and the parmigiano, which give this dish its unique taste.

1 small head cauliflower

1 pound carrots, peeled and sliced into $1/4$-inch rounds

4 tablespoons unsalted butter

1 large onion, thinly sliced

$1/2$ cup heavy cream

$1/3$ teaspoon freshly grated nutmeg

Salt

$1/2$ cup freshly grated Parmigiano-Reggiano

Butter for the baking dish

1. Remove all the leaves from the cauliflower and detach the florets. Wash florets under cold running water.

2. Bring two medium saucepans, each half full of water, to a boil over medium heat. Add cauliflower florets to one and carrots to the other. Cook, uncovered, until florets and carrots are tender but still a bit firm to the bite, 3 to 4 minutes for cauliflower and 4 to 5 minutes for carrots. Drain vegetables, cool under cold running water, and pat dry with paper towels. Place them in a large bowl until ready to use.

3. Heat 2 tablespoons of the butter in a medium skillet over medium heat. When the butter foams, add the onion, and cook, stirring occasionally, until pale yellow and soft, 5 to 6 minutes. Add onion to the bowl with cauliflower and carrots. Stir in the cream and nutmeg. Season with salt. Place vegetables in a buttered baking dish making sure they fit tightly together. Sprinkle Parmigiano over all and dot with the remaining butter.

4. Preheat the oven to 400°F. Place the baking dish in the oven and bake 20 to 25 minutes or until the top of the vegetables is lightly golden. Remove from oven and let the gratin stand 5 to 6 minutes before serving. *Makes 6 servings.*

Prepare ahead
Through step 3, several hours ahead. Cover and refrigerate.
Preheat oven and complete step 4 just before serving.

SAUTÉED MUSHROOM CAPS WITH BALSAMIC VINEGAR

When dishes are so remarkably simple and taste this good, it is exhilarating. The mushrooms are sautéed whole to a nice golden-brown color. The garlic is browned and then removed, so that only the hint of its flavor lingers on. The balsamic vinegar works its magic by enveloping the golden mushrooms.

3 to 4 tablespoons olive oil	**$^1/_4$ cup balsamic vinegar**
2 whole garlic cloves, peeled	**2 tablespoons minced chives**
1 pound white cultivated mushrooms, wiped clean with a damp towel	**Salt**

1. Heat the oil in a medium skillet over medium heat. Add the garlic cloves and cook until the garlic is golden brown. Discard the garlic.

2. Raise the heat to high and add the mushrooms. Cook until mushrooms are golden brown, 2 to 3 minutes. Take skillet off the heat and discard half of the oil.

3. Put the skillet back on high and add the balsamic vinegar and the chives. Season lightly with salt. Cook, stirring, until the vinegar is all reduced and the mushrooms are nicely glazed, 1 to 2 minutes. Serve at once. *Makes 4 to 6 servings.*

Prepare ahead
Through step 2, about one hour ahead.
Complete step 3 just before serving.

LOVING DINNERS FOR FRIENDS

Desserts

Baked Stuffed Apricots

Raspberries with Sparkling Wine Zabaglione

Medley of Grilled Fruit

Baked Lemon Custard with Raspberry Sauce

Fresh Berry Tart

Apple, Prune, and Grand Marnier Turnovers

Honey Bread Pudding

Hazelnut Shortcake

Almond, Date, Chocolate Honey Cake

BAKED STUFFED APRICOTS

This recipe, which draws its inspiration from the classic Italian "Baked Peaches," should not be considered an end in itself. Try it with pears or large, ripe plums. Change the filling to suit your mood, and a whole new category of desserts will be at your fingertips. If you are in the mood for something richer, serve the apricots over soft vanilla ice cream or over a pool of delicious golden zabaglione.

"Amaretti di Saronno" are delicious imported Italian cookies made with almonds that are available in most Italian markets and specialty food stores.

$^1/_3$ **cup sugar**

$^1/_2$ **cup shelled walnuts, minced**

8 Amaretti di Saronno cookies or almond cookies finely crumbled

$^1/_4$ **cup raspberry or strawberry jam**

3 to 4 tablespoons brandy

1$^1/_2$ pounds firm ripe apricots, washed, halved, and pitted

2 tablespoons unsalted butter, cut into small pieces

1. Preheat oven to 375°F. Generously butter a large baking dish.

2. In a small bowl, combine sugar, walnuts, cookie crumbs, jam, and brandy, and mix well. Spoon mixture into apricot cavities and place them filled sides up in the baking dish. Top each apricot with a bit of butter.

3. Bake until apricots are tender, 15 to 20 minutes. Transfer them to a serving platter and serve warm or at room temperature. *Makes 4 to 6 servings.*

Prepare ahead
Through step 3, several hours ahead.
To serve apricots warm, reheat them in a moderately warm oven just before serving.

RASPBERRIES WITH SPARKLING WINE ZABAGLIONE

When fresh raspberries are out of season, serve this fluffy, light zabaglione over poached pears, baked pears or baked apples. It is also delicious next to or over a slice of Hazelnut Shortcake, page 140, or Honey Bread Pudding, page 139. Zabaglione is a traditional Italian sauce.

8 large egg yolks at room temperature	**1 cup heavy cream, beaten to medium-stiff consistency**
$^1/_2$ cup sugar	**2 pints fresh raspberries**
1 cup sparkling wine	

1. In a large bowl or in the top part of a double boiler, with an electric mixer or large wire whisk, beat the egg yolks with the sugar until thick and pale yellow. Set the bowl or top of the double boiler over simmering water. Add the wine slowly, beating after each addition. (Do not let the water boil or you will cook the eggs.) Cook and beat vigorously until zabaglione has doubled in volume, is soft, fluffy, and hot to the touch, 4 to 6 minutes.

2. Place the bowl with the zabaglione over a larger bowl of ice water and stir until cool. Fold the whipped cream into the zabaglione. Cover the bowl and refrigerate until ready to use.

3. Put some zabaglione into large glasses, top with the berries, drizzle more zabaglione over the berries and serve. *Makes 6 servings.*

Prepare ahead
Through step 2, several hours to a day ahead.
Complete step 3 at the last moment, or an hour or so before serving.

MEDLEY OF GRILLED FRUIT

If using a broiler instead of a grill or barbecue, place fruit, cut side up, on a broiler pan. Sprinkle with sugar, and place under the broiler, 2 to 3 inches from the heat source. When nicely browned, turn to brown the other side.

In Winter

3 green apples, with skin on, halved and cored

3 bananas, peeled and halved lengthwise

3 Bosc pears, with skin on, halved and cored

In Summer

3 large peaches, halved and cored

6 apricots, halved and cored

6 plums, halved and cored

3 bananas, peeled and halved lengthwise

2 to 3 tablespoons unsalted butter, melted

Grand Marnier or Amaretto di Saronno liqueur (optional)

1/2 cup brown sugar

1. Preheat the grill or the barbecue until hot.

2. Brush the cut sides of the fruit with the melted butter and sprinkle evenly with half of the sugar. Place fruit, cut sides down, over the hot grill. Grill until the fruit is golden brown and a bit soft, then turn to grill the other side.

3. Transfer fruit to a platter and drizzle with a bit more butter and the remaining sugar. If desired, sprinkle with a bit of Grand Marnier. Serve warm. *Makes 6 servings.*

Prepare ahead
Apples and pears can be sliced and cored ahead of time and can be kept in a bowl of cold water with lemon juice to prevent discoloring. Grill the fruit just before serving.

TIP: When using summer fruit, try to select fruit that is ripe but still a bit firm to the touch. Keep your eyes on the fruit as it cooks, for it can easily overcook.

◀ Medley of Grilled Fruit

BAKED LEMON CUSTARD WITH RASPBERRY SAUCE

A properly prepared custard should have a smooth texture and a tender, delicate consistency. Unmold custards just before you serve, letting the golden caramel flow over and down the sides of the custards. If the caramel is too firm and it is difficult to unmold the custard, briefly dip mold halfway in a bowl of hot water, dry the mold, and turn onto the plate.

For the Custard

3 cups milk	**2 large egg yolks**
1 vanilla bean	**³/4 cup sugar**
Grated peel of 1 lemon	**Juice of 1 lemon**
6 large eggs	

For the Caramel Syrup

1 cup sugar	**¹/2 cup water**

For the Raspberry Sauce

2 pints fresh raspberries	**Juice of ¹/2 lemon**
¹/4 cup sugar	

1. *Prepare the custard:* Heat the milk with the vanilla bean and lemon peel in a medium saucepan over medium heat. In a medium bowl, lightly mix the eggs, egg yolks, and sugar with a whisk. (Do not beat or you will incorporate too much air and will create foam.) Add the warm milk to the eggs very slowly, a little at a time, mixing gently after each addition. Transfer the mixture back into the saucepan and place over medium-low heat. Cook and stir, without letting the milk boil, for 4 to 5 minutes. Discard the vanilla bean and strain the custard into a clean bowl. Stir in the lemon juice.

2. *Prepare the caramel:* Combine the sugar and the water in a small, heavy skillet, and cook over high heat, stirring, until the sugar is completely dissolved. Cook without stirring until the mixture has a golden brown color and a syrupy-thick consistency, 3 to 4 minutes. Pour the syrup into 6 individual 1-cup round molds or ramekins, tilting the molds to coat sides and bottoms. This step should be done quickly because the syrup will set quickly. Cool the molds 10 to 15 minutes and then pour the custard into the molds.

3. Preheat oven to 325°F. Place the molds in a deep baking dish and pour just enough hot water into the dish to come ³/₄ of the way up the sides of the molds. Bake 1 to 1¹/₄ hours, or until a thin knife inserted into the custards comes out clean. Cool custards 1 hour, then refrigerate until ready to use.

4. *Prepare the raspberry sauce:* Put raspberries, sugar, and lemon juice in a blender or in the bowl of a food processor fitted with the metal blade, and process into a thick sauce. Press the sauce through a sieve into a bowl. Cover and set aside until ready to use.

5. When you are ready to serve, run a thin knife around each custard to detach from the mold. Place a flat serving plate over the mold and invert the custard. Pat gently and lift up the mold. The custard will have a nice brown glazing of caramel over the top and the sides. Unmold remaining custards. Spoon raspberry sauce all around the custards and serve. *Makes 6 servings.*

Prepare ahead
Through step 4, several hours to a day ahead.
Complete step 5 just before serving.

Cooking is a way of giving.
—Michel Bourdin

FRESH BERRY TART

In winter, prepare this tart with pears. Peel and halve 3 large Bosc pears, and simmer them slowly in white wine and sugar until tender. Drain pears on paper towels. Arrange them, cut sides down, over the pastry cream, no more than one half hour before serving.

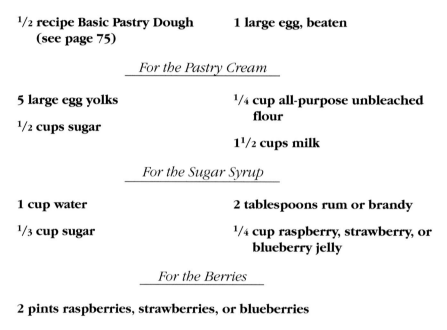

¹/₂ recipe Basic Pastry Dough (see page 75)   **1 large egg, beaten**

For the Pastry Cream

5 large egg yolks   **¹/₄ cup all-purpose unbleached flour**

¹/₂ cups sugar   **1¹/₂ cups milk**

For the Sugar Syrup

1 cup water   **2 tablespoons rum or brandy**

¹/₃ cup sugar   **¹/₄ cup raspberry, strawberry, or blueberry jelly**

For the Berries

2 pints raspberries, strawberries, or blueberries

1. Prepare the Basic Pastry Dough, and refrigerate until ready to use.

2. Preheat the oven to 400°F. Butter an 8-inch tart pan with a removable bottom.

3. On a lightly-floured surface, roll out the dough to a 10-inch thin round. Carefully place the dough in the buttered tart pan, pressing gently to fit the bottom and sides. Trim the edges of dough by gently pressing the rolling pin over the top of the pan. Prick the bottom of the pastry shell in several places with a fork. Line the pastry shell with aluminum foil and fill the foil with uncooked rice or beans. (This will prevent the pastry from shrinking while baking.) Bake 12 to 15 minutes then remove the foil. Brush dough with a beaten egg and return pastry shell to the oven until golden brown, 7 to 8 minutes. Cool to room temperature.

4. *Prepare Pastry Cream:* In a large bowl, beat the egg yolks and sugar by hand or with an electric beater or wire whisk, until mixture is pale yellow. Slowly beat in the flour.

5. In a medium saucepan, heat the milk short of a boil. Slowly pour the hot milk into the egg mixture, stirring constantly with a wooden spoon. Pour milk/egg mixture back into the saucepan and cook over medium heat, stirring constantly and scraping all around the bottom and sides of the pan until mixture begins to thicken, 4 to 5 minutes. (Do not let the mixture come to a boil, but allow a very gentle, slow simmer.) When done, the pastry cream should have a medium-thick, smooth consistency. Transfer it to a clean bowl. Chill in the refrigerator for a few hours to allow the pastry cream to become firm.

6. *Prepare the Sugar Syrup:* In a small skillet, combine the water, sugar, rum, and jelly. Cook over low heat, stirring a few times, until the sugar is dissolved and the mixture has a medium-thick consistency, 3 to 4 minutes.

7. Fill the bottom of the tart shell evenly with the chilled pastry cream, and arrange the berries tightly together over the cream. Brush berries lightly with the syrup. Cool before serving. *Makes 6 servings.*

Prepare ahead

Through step 3, several hours or a few days ahead. It can be stored tightly wrapped in the refrigerator or in the freezer.

Steps 4 and 5, several hours or a day or two ahead. Keep it tightly covered in the refrigerator.

Complete the tart, steps 6 and 7, one or two hours before serving.

All culinary tasks should be performed with reverential love.
—Norman Douglas

APPLE, PRUNE, AND GRAND MARNIER TURNOVERS

Commercially-made unbaked pie crust can be substituted for the Basic Pastry Dough.

1 recipe **Basic Pastry Dough** (see page 75)

1/2 **pound pitted prunes, coarsely chopped**

3 **tablespoons Grand Marnier or brandy**

2 **tablespoons unsalted butter**

3 **large apples, peeled, cored, and thinly sliced**

1/4 **cup honey**

1/3 **cup sugar**

1 **large egg, beaten in a small bowl**

Sugar for topping

1. Prepare Basic Pastry Dough, shape into a ball, and refrigerate for one hour. Line a baking sheet with parchment paper (if you don't have parchment paper, just generously butter the baking sheet).

2. Put the prunes and the Grand Marnier in the bowl of a food processor fitted with the metal blade and process into small pieces.

3. Heat the butter in a medium skillet over medium heat. Add the apples and cook, stirring, until tender, 4 to 5 minutes. Add the prunes, honey, and sugar, and cook until the mixture has a thick, glazed consistency, 2 to 3 minutes. Transfer to a bowl and cool to room temperature.

4. Preheat the oven to 400°F. On a lightly-floured surface, roll out the dough into a large, thin round and cut it into six, 6-inch rounds. Place rounds on the baking sheet and spoon some fruit mixture into the center of each round. Fold the dough over the filling so that the edges meet. Fold the edges slightly to form a 1/2-inch border, then pinch the border with your fingertips or with a fork to seal. Brush the turnovers with the beaten egg and sprinkle with sugar. Bake 15 to 20 minutes or until pastry is golden brown. Serve warm or at room temperature. *Makes 6 servings.*

Prepare ahead
Through step 4, several hours ahead.
For warm turnovers, reheat briefly in a moderately hot oven just before serving.

HONEY BREAD PUDDING

8 to 10 (^{1}/$_2$-inch thick) slices
crusty Italian bread, preferably
one to two days old, with crust
removed

^{1}/$_4$ pound (1 stick) unsalted
butter

^{1}/$_2$ cup honey

^{1}/$_3$ cup dark rum

^{1}/$_2$ cup golden raisins, soaked in
lukewarm water for 20
minutes, then drained

4 large eggs

^{1}/$_2$ cup sugar

1 cup heavy cream

3 cups milk

1. Preheat the oven to 375°F. Generously butter a 9 × 12-inch baking dish. Arrange the bread slices in a single layer in the dish, slightly overlapping each other. Set aside.

2. Melt the butter in a small saucepan over medium-low heat. Add the honey and rum, and raise the heat to high. Cook, stirring, until sauce begins to thicken and is foamy and bubbling, 3 to 4 minutes. Stir in the raisins, remove from heat, and pour over the bread evenly.

3. In a medium bowl, beat the eggs with ^{1}/$_3$ cup of the sugar. Add the cream and milk, and beat well to combine. Pour over the bread and sprinkle with remaining sugar.

4. Bake 15 minutes, then reduce the heat to 325°F and bake an additional 20 to 25 minutes, or until pudding is set and the bread has a nice golden color. Remove pudding from oven, and let it stand. Cool to room temperature and serve. *Makes 6 servings.*

Prepare ahead
Through step 4, several hours or a day or two ahead. Cover and refrigerate.
If pudding is refrigerated, allow it to come to room temperature before serving.

HAZELNUT SHORTCAKE

I love desserts that can be put together with such little effort and taste as delicious as this hazelnut shortcake. A shortcake is extremely versatile. It can be served alone or with fresh berries, fruit compote, whipped cream, mousse, cream sauce, or ice cream.

1 cup hazelnuts	$^1/_2$ cup granulated sugar
1$^1/_2$ cups all-purpose unbleached flour	5 large eggs
2 teaspoons baking powder	Grated peel of 1 lemon
$^1/_4$ pound (1 stick) unsalted butter	$^1/_3$ cup heavy cream
	$^1/_4$ cup confectioners' sugar

1. Preheat the oven to 350°F. Butter and flour an 8-inch springform cake pan.

2. Put the hazelnuts in an ungreased shallow baking pan and bake until they are lightly golden, 3 to 4 minutes. Wrap them in a kitchen towel and rub off as much skin as possible. Chop the hazelnuts in a food processor into small granular pieces, pulsing the machine on and off. Do not process into powder.

3. In a medium bowl, combine hazelnuts, flour, and baking powder. Set aside.

4. Put butter and granulated sugar in the bowl of an electric mixer and beat at medium speed to blend. Beat in the eggs, one at a time. Beat in lemon peel and cream. Add flour-hazelnut mixture in two to three batches and beat at low speed to incorporate. At this point, the batter should be fairly soft and a bit runny. Pour batter into the baking pan, shaking it a few times to spread the batter evenly, and then level the top with a spatula. Bake until the top of the cake is golden brown and a thin knife inserted in the center of the cake comes out clean, 30 to 35 minutes. Cool cake on a wire rack to room temperature. Place cake on a serving platter, sprinkle with confectioners' sugar, and serve. *Makes 6 servings.*

Prepare ahead
Through step 4, several hours or a day ahead.

ALMOND, DATE, CHOCOLATE HONEY CAKE

6 ounces blanched whole or slivered almonds

³/₄ pound pitted dates

2 to 3 tablespoons dark rum

4 ounces semisweet chocolate, grated

¹/₂ to ³/₄ cup honey

4 large eggs, beaten

2 large egg whites, beaten to a stiff consistency with 1 tablespoon of sugar

1. Preheat the oven to 350°F. Butter and flour an 8-inch springform cake pan.

2. Put the almonds on a baking sheet and bake until lightly golden, 2 to 3 minutes. Place almonds in the bowl of a food processor and chop them into very small pieces. (Be careful not to process them into powder.) Transfer almonds to a large bowl and set aside.

3. Put the dates and the rum in the food processor (no need to clean the bowl of the almond residue), and chop into very fine pieces.

4. Add the chopped dates, chocolate, honey, and 4 beaten eggs to the bowl with the almonds, and mix thoroughly. (The mixture should have a fairly soft, loose consistency. If too firm, add one additional egg or a bit more rum.) Thoroughly fold the egg whites into the mixture and pour it into the buttered cake pan. Shake the pan lightly to distribute the batter evenly and level the top with a spatula.

5. Bake 40 to 50 minutes, or until the cake is golden brown and a thin knife inserted in the center of the cake comes out just slightly moist. Cool to room temperature and serve. *Makes 6 servings.*

Prepare ahead
Through step 5, several hours or a few days ahead. Cover and refrigerate.

LOVING DINNERS FOR FAMILY

"We live in an age of convenience foods and household appliances. We do not have to slaughter pigs, pluck chickens, or make soap and candles. We do not handwash clothes. Machines often wash our dishes for us—and still everyone complains that they hardly have any time. The American family, we are told, is falling apart. It does not dine: it grazes from snack to snack."

—Laurie Colwin

The Care and Feeding of Family

Family is not a luxury. It is a necessity for physical and mental development and happiness. The dictionary defines a family as "a social unit consisting of parents and the children they rear." Robert Frost, with tongue in cheek, defines it as a place that "when you go there they have to take you in." I offer another definition. To me, the family is the ever dynamic social structure upon which lives are built. "Family" was where I learned to love, to commit, to communicate, to share, to compromise. "Family" was where I felt the warmth, the security and safety in which to experiment with my life. I had no illusions that mine was the perfect family, but from the imperfections I learned to make my choices and take the responsibility for them.

There can be no doubt that of all my life's experiences, those involving my family have remained the most memorable, significant, and influential.

When I think of family I always think of Sundays. Sunday was family day in our home. Together we went to church for early Mass and then eagerly raced back to read the Sunday papers and for what we knew would be a memorable experience, because Sunday was Papa's day in the kitchen. Not that we didn't love Mama's cooking, but we experienced her meals daily. They were more basic. Papa's Sunday meals were more exotic and subtle. They took inordinate amounts of preparation and were beautifully presented. It was only on Sundays that we sampled such exotic dishes as escargot, pheasant, grouper, veal rolatini, stuffed uccellini, and mushroom-filled ravioli.

Attendance at Papa's dinners was mandatory. No excuses for being elsewhere were accepted. But who wanted to be elsewhere? I recall Mama sitting regally in her special chair in the living room, reading her missal or the Italian newspaper, often stopping to take time to converse with her beloved *bambini*, and generally reveling in her day off.

Papa was a true diplomat. He realized that he was usurping Mama's domain, and, even though it was his kitchen on Sundays, he always asked for Mama's opinion. Should he add a bit of salt to this, a little basil to that?

Should the pasta be cooked a bit longer? We would watch enthralled as Mama tasted, smacked her lips, cogitated for a while like a wine connoisseur over a special vintage, then gave her opinion—a bit more cheese, a touch of fresh oregano, a few seconds, no more, for the pasta to become *al dente*. We all knew beforehand that nothing would ever be exactly right for Mama, but Papa would take her comments with good humor and return to his labor of love.

It was on Sundays that the oil cloth was removed from the dining room table and replaced with a linen one. Stemware took the place of the everyday jelly glasses. The fine china was brought out. A bowl of fresh flowers from Papa's endless garden was placed at the center of the table.

The antipasto was served as soon as we were all seated. Papa arranged it with the attention of an artist: cooked peppers fanned in red, yellow, and green, varieties of dried salamis, marinated vegetables, tomatoes, onions, and mushrooms—all succulent with virgin olive oil and wine vinegar and accompanied with crispy, crusty Italian bread.

The pasta course that followed was always a surprise. We were continually amazed by the endless varieties of noodle dishes—*paglia e fieno, lasagne, rigatoni, orecchiette, manicotti*. Each and every one was a favorite. What Papa could do with an inexpensive piece of meat or fish was miraculous. Some herbs, some garlic, a splash of wine, and magic was assured.

A leafy salad of fresh greens from the garden always followed, with creative and tasty dressings, which Papa developed on the spot, handling the oil and vinegar bottles like a circus juggler. After this would arrive the favorite moment for us children—the dessert! A meal was never complete without something rich and sweet like zabaglione, floating island, flan, cake, or fruit tarts.

What made Papa's Sunday meal especially exciting was the family lingering around the table in animated conversation. In addition, we were all, no matter our age, allowed to taste a drop of wine. A splash of nectar in a crystal goblet! Magic! Papa was convinced that the way to avoid creating an alcoholic was to treat spirits matter-of-factly, yet respectfully. He used this weekly ritual to give us our wine appreciation course, explaining the variety, the color, the nose, all of the various qualities that made it unique.

Papa and Mama, of course, are long gone, but they've left me with a deep appreciation for family and Sunday dinners. Now, while preparing them, my mind wanders to those happy days that are very much alive and vividly etched in memory. Nostalgia has become an important ingredient to these dinners, mixed with equal parts aroma, taste, animation, laughter, and love. How sad that so many today will never know the joy of a family gathered together around a table laden with the staff of life and the essence of love.

Over the years, these rich memories have served me well. They have enhanced my faith in the importance of the past and strengthened my belief in the future. They have reinforced my determination to withstand those insidious daily pressures that might, in some way, endanger my love of family or family ties.

I am amused and astonished each time I am brave enough to suggest that we "get the family together." A house full of aunts, uncles, brothers, sisters, nephews, and nieces has the potential to become a very volatile situation. "*Fete de famille*? Forget it!" they all agree, "Better a slow, painful death!" All are quick to relate their favorite horror stories of past family debacles and gastronomic nightmares. They whole-heartedly agree with M.F.K. Fisher who wrote in her wonderful book, *An Alphabet For Gourmets*: "The cold truth is that family dinners are more often than not an ordeal of nervous indigestion, preceded by hidden resentment and ennui and accompanied by psychosomatic jitters. The best way to guarantee smooth sailing at one of them is to assemble relatives only when a will must be read."

Everyone seems to have a different leading character reinforcing the dread of family gatherings. There is brother Wally, a gentle vegetarian, who becomes violent when the meat course is served. There is sister Carol, who counts calories with a calculator and accuses everyone of gluttony. Who can ignore Anna Maria, always the first at the table and the last to leave, who gives the expression "second helping" another meaning?

Uncle Joe, who can't wait to get an audience in order to air his views on religion, politics, and the imminent fall of Western civilization, while Aunt Mary tries desperately to outdo him with her horror stories of recent operations and illnesses. Dear Aunt Winona, who is quick to state that she is never hungry. (She only eats food if it comes from someone else's plate.) And Uncle Tony, who is notorious for reinforcing the old adage that practicing alcoholics are never anonymous.

So it is really no surprise that even so much as a mention of these family gatherings can bring on emotional and physical distress requiring pro-longed trips to local spas or voyages to the healing waters of Lourdes—anywhere far from "the dear relatives."

And so the family tables remain empty, sadly becoming a vague, sentimental memory, relegated to the "good ol' days." The implication is that we may love our relatives, but we don't like them enough to spend an evening sharing food with them.

Yet I am still convinced of the positive values of frequent family dinners. Happy laughter and voices joyously raised over a good meal have the potential for keeping more kids off the streets, more couples out of divorce courts, and preventing more unhappiness and conflict than any other therapeutic activity. We often miss these experiences simply because we have never taken the time, or because they conjure up fears of chaos and past negative experiences that may no longer be appropriate.

It has been found that the more secure we are as a member of a family group, the better we feel about ourselves and the more we are willing to risk expanding our lives. The family remains a safe place to practice the wonders and possibilities of life. Family love may be old, but often we do not explore and reinforce it enough for it to show the positive signs of age.

When I think of my childhood, it seems as if every significant moment in the lives of the eleven people who made up our family happened around the heavy, deeply-stained, ornately-carved table that was Papa's pride and joy. I never recall the dining area being idle. Mama kept the table covered with a large oil cloth with an ostentatiously bright pattern of colors, which was always in the process of being cleaned, set, dismantled, or readied for some event. Eleven family members of all ages, shapes, and sizes, sitting at the table, eagerly sharing in a common activity—eating. Eleven individuals surrendering to companionship, conversation, and love: a stage set for miracles.

The kitchen, which was adjacent to this dining area, was a place of unceasing movement. It seemed as if someone was constantly engaged in a food-related activity there, no matter the time of day or night. I have the memory of food being brought in, put away, cleaned, washed, marinated, baked, steamed, boiled, seasoned, mixed, kneaded, or "sampled." Hands were always in action—cutting, dicing, puréeing, mixing, and slicing. Then, suddenly, "*Ecco!*"—something wonderful would be presented: a platter of gnocchi, a stuffed veal roast, steamed squash, or a savory tart.

Mama's agile hands, like Tinkerbell's wand, spread magic over everything. It also was in the kitchen where we were introduced to her favorite Puccini and Verdi arias, as she hummed and sang while creating the day's nourishment. It was love in action. Food was love, and its preparation, presentation, and sharing, were her manifestations of it.

Mama was convinced that eating well was the answer to any problem, from anxiety to zoophobia. "Eat now, cry later," was her motto. "There's nothing wrong with you that a good pasta can't cure. Take something hot, a bowl of minestrone soup." Her words of healing were words of love.

Food in our house was more than just something to eat. Take Mama's minestrone soup, for example. It was a symbol of security, goodness, and health. It served as an economic gauge, a unifier, and an expression of love that was tangible. And, it stuck to the ribs!

I can still see the soup pot sitting on the stove in all its chipped, white-and-blue enameled glory, its contents always simmering, steam rising as from an active volcano. As I came home from school, I could smell the soup from the street. When I entered the back porch, the smell was not only mouth watering, but reassuring. Whether Mama was standing over the pot stirring with a long wooden spoon or not, I knew that I was home.

There was really no recipe for her minestrone soup. I remember that it would start with some water and a bag of meat bones that she usually got for nothing from the butcher. (She was outraged when he later began to charge her a few pennies for them.) Once the water was simmering, she would add vegetables: onions, tomatoes, cabbage, carrots, beans, peas, and eventually pastas of various shapes and sizes. As with all recipes Mama cooked, I always suspected that there was a special secret ingredient. In this case, I noticed that when the soup began to lose its flavor, or became too thick, she would add a generous splash of wine, stir it, and leave it to continue its slow, gentle simmer. We could always judge the state of our family economy by the state of the soup. A thick brew indicated that things were going well with the Buscaglias; a watery soup denoted meager times. But at no time was food ever thrown out. Everything ended up in the minestrone pot.

Minestrone was medicinal, too, serving both physical and emotional needs. Any time was soup time. If Papa worked late—and his job as a waiter made this happen more often than not—Mama would get out of bed in her cotton bathrobe, her long brown hair falling in waves over her shoulders, and pour him a bowl of soup. She counted his tips and listened while he ate and told her of the trials and tribulations or joys and successes of the day.

If we got hurt, Mama's remedy was always a hug and a bowl of soup. This prescription cured colds, fever, headaches, indigestion, heartaches, and loneliness.

When people dropped in, strangers included, they would soon find themselves gathered around the kitchen table, talking over a bowl of steaming soup. It was an act of communion.

Mama died a long time ago. Things were never the same after that. Someone turned off the gas under the minestrone pot the day after she was buried, and a whole era passed with the flame. Oh, we still make minestrone from time to time, but in smaller quantities, and only on special occasions. The continual warmth and assurance with which it once filled the house is somehow missing.

Fast foods, harried schedules, and more sedentary lifestyles have all lessened the joy of the family table. Cooking for most people has become simply a necessity, the main purpose being to allay hunger before rushing off to "matters of consequence." I have been told that, among the many changes taking place in Europe, there is a mass invasion of fast and frozen foods, an abandoning of the kitchen, and the age-old ritual of the family dinners. I am pleased to report that this is an exaggerated observation. I noticed on my last European trip that many things have, indeed, changed, but not the importance of food and family dining.

Not too long ago, I visited a small family-run Swiss restaurant. Here the proprietor and his robust wife served as chef, sommelier, waiter, bus boy, and cashier. Two diners at the table next to ours were very audibly stewing over the length of time it was taking for each course to emerge from the kitchen. They finally complained angrily to the owner. His reaction was one of incredulity.

Collecting himself, he informed them, "This is a restaurant. People come here to 'dine', if you want to 'eat', go to McDonald's." Having said this, he swept grandly back into his kitchen.

True dining is an experience available to us all. Unlike many things in life that seem the sole prerogative of the fortunate few, anyone can create the proper ambiance for a dining experience. It requires only a desire to enhance, to please, to share the best that life has to offer. It claims only a little time, a dabble of creativity, a shopping bag of fresh ingredients, a pinch of herbs, a splash of wine, lots of love, and like magic, the scene is set for wonder!

LOVING DINNERS FOR FAMILY

Starters

Vegetable Soup with Rice

Thai Chicken Soup

Gazpacho

Spinach, Walnut, and Parmigiano Salad

Orange, Red Onion, and Green Olive Salad

Roasted Onion Salad with Balsamic Vinegar

Mussel and Clam Salad

White Bean and Smoked Salmon Salad

Savory Pizza with Sweet and Sour Onions

Bruschetta with Grilled Tomatoes and Pancetta

VEGETABLE SOUP WITH RICE

Every area of Italy has its own minestrone—vegetable soups that are redolent with the bounty of seasonal fresh vegetables and the skilled hands of the Italian cook. I wanted to include this minestrone which originates in the north of Italy, because Leo and I grew up with food like this. Good, honest, simple food, prepared exuberantly with an abundance of love.

The base of onion, pancetta, garlic, sage, and parsley, which in Italy is called battuto, enriches and binds the vegetables with a delightful flavor. This soup, like most hearty soups, becomes even better several hours after it has been made. Rice can be replaced by small tubular macaroni or with grilled or toasted bread. If you use grilled or toasted bread, place it in the soup bowls and top with the soup, then add the parmesan. For a lighter soup, omit rice or bread and serve at room temperature, perhaps adding a few drops of extra-virgin olive oil to each serving.

$^1/_3$ **cup olive oil**

1 small onion, finely minced

$^1/_4$ **pound pancetta, finely minced**

3 garlic cloves, finely minced

2 tablespoons chopped fresh parsley

2 medium carrots, diced

2 celery stalks, diced

2 medium potatoes, peeled and diced

$^1/_4$ **pound white cultivated mushrooms, diced**

$^1/_4$ **pound green beans with ends removed, diced**

$^1/_2$ **pound small zucchini with ends removed, diced**

$^1/_2$ **of a small savoy or regular cabbage, diced**

10 cups chicken broth or water

1 cup canned imported Italian tomatoes with their juice, roughly cut into small pieces

Salt and freshly ground pepper

1 cup uncooked rice, preferably imported Italian arborio rice or short grain California pearl rice

1 pound fresh peas, shelled, or 1 cup frozen peas, thawed

$^1/_2$ **cup freshly grated parmesan**

1. Heat the oil in a large soup pot over medium heat. Add the onion, pancetta, garlic, and parsley. Cook, stirring, until onion is pale yellow and soft, 5 to 6 minutes.

2. Add all the vegetables, except the peas, to the onion mixture. Stir thoroughly. Add broth and tomatoes. Season with salt and pepper. Bring the liquid to a boil, then reduce the heat to low, cover the pot, and simmer the soup 1 to $1^1/_2$ hours. Stir a few times during cooking.

3. Add the rice and peas and simmer, stirring occasionally, 8 to 10 minutes. The rice should still be a bit firm because it will finish cooking in the hot soup. Turn off the heat and leave the soup on the stove until ready to use. Serve soup with a generous sprinkling of freshly grated parmesan. *Makes 10 servings.*

Prepare ahead

Through step 3, several hours or a few days ahead. If prepared a few days ahead, do not add the rice and peas. Keep the soup tightly covered in the refrigerator. Just before serving reheat the soup gently over moderate heat, add the rice and peas and cook until it is al dente.

TIP: Pancetta is Italian bacon, but unlike bacon, pancetta is not smoked but is cured in salt and spices. Pancetta is widely available in Italian markets and in specialty stores. If unavailable in your area, substitute with Canadian bacon or with regular American bacon. If you are using American bacon, briefly plunge the slices in some boiling water to remove some of the fat; then, dice the bacon, mince it, and proceed as instructed in the recipe.

THAI CHICKEN SOUP

Lemon grass, a member of the "Graminae" grass family, is an important element of Asian cooking. The long, stiff stalks have a gray-green color and a pungent, lemony aroma.

To use lemon grass, remove the woody top part of the stalks and peel the fibrous outer layers. Slice the pale, tubular core of the stalks very thinly, and use as instructed in the recipe.

4 tablespoons corn oil

1 medium onion, thinly sliced

4 garlic cloves, thinly sliced

2-inch piece of fresh ginger, peeled and minced

8 cups chicken broth

2 stalks lemon grass, prepared as above

1 to 2 teaspoons chili pepper flakes

2 cups coconut milk

2 medium chicken breasts, boned, skinned, and cut into 1-inch strips

4 ounces sliced water chestnuts, drained

4 ounces bamboo shoots, drained

Salt

Juice of 1 lime

8 to 10 fresh basil leaves, thinly sliced

1. Heat the oil in a medium saucepan over medium heat. Add the onion and cook, stirring, until it is pale yellow, 5 to 6 minutes. Add the garlic and ginger. Stir about one minute. Add broth, lemon grass, and pepper flakes. Bring broth to a boil, then reduce the heat to low and simmer, uncovered, 30 to 40 minutes.

2. Add the coconut milk, chicken, water chestnuts, and bamboo shoots. Simmer 10 to 15 minutes longer. Lightly season with salt. Remove from heat and stir in the lime juice and basil. Ladle soup into bowls, and serve. *Makes 6 to 8 servings.*

Prepare ahead
Through step 2, several hours ahead. Cover and refrigerate.
Reheat the soup gently, stirring in lime juice and basil just before serving.

TIP: Lemon grass and canned coconut milk are available in Asian markets.

◀ Thai Chicken Soup

GAZPACHO

Perhaps there is no other soup so perfect for a hot summer day as gazpacho. This great uncooked Spanish soup takes advantage of the summer bounty and allows the chef freedom to add and improvise at whim. For a fresh-tasting, fragrant gazpacho, try to use it the day you have made it. Leftover gazpacho can be frozen.

4 pounds firm ripe tomatoes

4 slices Italian or French bread, ¹/₂-inch thick, crust removed

¹/₂ to ³/₄ cup sherry vinegar or red wine vinegar

1 large onion, diced

4 garlic cloves, minced

3 medium cucumbers, peeled, seeded, and diced

2 large red bell peppers, halved, cored, seeded, and diced

1 cup loosely packed parsley leaves, roughly chopped

10 large, fresh basil leaves, roughly chopped

Salt and freshly ground pepper

¹/₂ cup olive oil

2 to 3 cups chicken or vegetable broth

¹/₄ cup finely minced onion or cucumber for garnish

1. Bring a large pot of water to a boil over high heat. Add tomatoes and cook just until skins begin to split, about one minute. Transfer tomatoes to a bowl of cold water. Peel, seed, and dice tomatoes roughly, and place in a large bowl.

2. Break the bread into small pieces, place in a small bowl with the vinegar, and soak for a few minutes. Add onion, garlic, cucumbers, bell peppers, parsley, basil, and soaked bread to the bowl with the tomatoes. Season with salt and pepper and toss with olive oil. Cover the bowl and refrigerate for a few hours.

3. Put gazpacho, in several batches, in the bowl of a food processor fitted with the metal blade. Purée, pulsing the machine on and off. (Make sure not to purée into a cream. It should retain a coarse texture.) Transfer gazpacho to a large bowl and stir in broth as needed. Gazpacho should have a medium-thick consistency. Taste, adjust the seasoning, and refrigerate until ready to use. *Makes 8 to 10 servings.*

Prepare ahead
Through step 3, several hours or a day ahead.
Serve with a drizzle of olive oil and garnish each serving with a bit of minced onion or finely diced cucumbers.

SPINACH, WALNUT, AND PARMIGIANO SALAD

Trim and wash the spinach several hours ahead. Dry it well with paper towels, and keep it in a plastic bag in the refrigerator. However, to fully enjoy the spinach flavor, do not serve the salad too cold, just barely chilled.

2¹/₂ **pounds fresh spinach**

3 **ounces shelled walnuts**

¹/₄ **cup red wine vinegar**

¹/₂ **tablespoon mild Dijon mustard**

¹/₃ **to** ¹/₂ **cup olive oil, preferably extra-virgin**

Salt and freshly ground pepper

2 **to** 3 **ounces very thinly sliced parmigiano**

1. Remove the stems from the spinach. Wash the leaves thoroughly under cold running water. Pat them dry with paper towels and place in a large salad bowl.

2. Preheat the oven to 350°F. Place the walnuts on an ungreased baking sheet and toast until they are lightly golden, 2 to 3 minutes.

3. In a small bowl, combine the vinegar and mustard and beat with a fork or a small wire whisk to incorporate. Add the olive oil slowly and mix well to blend.

4. Season the spinach with salt and pepper, and dress with the oil/mustard mixture. Taste and adjust the seasoning. Put the salad into individual serving dishes, top with the roasted walnuts and the thinly sliced parmesan, and serve. *Makes 6 to 8 servings.*

Prepare ahead
Through step 3, several hours ahead (see note).
Dress the salad, step 4, just before serving.

ORANGE, RED ONION, AND GREEN OLIVE SALAD

8 large oranges

1 medium red onion, very thinly sliced

3 to 4 ounces small pitted green olives, quartered

Salt and freshly ground black pepper

Juice of 1 large lemon

$1/4$ to $1/3$ cup olive oil, preferably extra-virgin

1. Peel the oranges taking care to remove all the white pith. Cut oranges into $1/4$-inch thick rounds and remove the seeds. Place on a platter, cover and refrigerate.

2. Fan out orange slices on individual serving dishes. Top oranges with onion and olives. Season with salt and pepper, and sprinkle with the lemon juice and olive oil. Serve slightly chilled. *Makes 8 servings.*

Prepare ahead
Through step 1, several hours ahead.
Step 2, one-half hour before serving.

Unless you live alone in a cave or hermitage, cooking and eating are social activities: even hermit monks have one communal meal a month. The sharing of food is the basis of social life, and to many people it is the only kind of social life worth participating in.
—Laurie Colwin

ROASTED ONION SALAD WITH BALSAMIC VINEGAR

$^1/_2$ **cup olive oil, preferably extra-virgin**

$^1/_4$ **cup balsamic vinegar, or red wine vinegar**

8 medium red onions (4 to 5 pounds) with root ends on, peeled and quartered

Salt and freshly ground pepper

1. Preheat the oven to 400°F. Combine the oil and vinegar in a large baking dish and add the onions. Turn onions several times to coat on all sides with the oil mixture. Season with salt and several twists of pepper. Bake until onions are golden brown and completely cooked, 50 to 60 minutes. Remove from oven and cool to room temperature.

2. Slice onions into strips and place in a salad bowl. Pour some of the pan juices over, taste, and adjust the seasoning. Serve at room temperature. *Makes 8 servings.*

Prepare ahead
Through step 2, several hours ahead.

Dining is a privilege of civilization.
—Isabella Beeton

MUSSEL AND CLAM SALAD

4 pounds mussels	**2 to 3 tablespoons minced chives**
4 pounds medium to small clams	**2 to 3 tablespoons capers, rinsed**
Salt	**$^1/_2$ small red onion, minced**
$^1/_2$ cup olive oil, preferably extra-virgin	**3 to 4 anchovy fillets, chopped (optional)**
2 cups dry white wine	**$^1/_2$ pound firm ripe tomatoes, halved, seeded, and diced**
Juice of 1 large lemon	
$^1/_4$ cup red wine vinegar	**Salt and freshly ground pepper**
2 garlic cloves, minced	**Slices of grilled or toasted bread**

1. Soak the mussels and clams in a large bowl of cold salted water, then wash and scrub them under cold running water, making sure to remove the "beard" of the mussels and any grit that is attached to the shells. (The "beard" of the mussels is the bundle of fibers that protrudes between the shells.)

2. Heat 2 tablespoons of the oil with the wine and lemon juice in a large deep skillet or saucepan over medium heat. Add the mussels and clams, and cover the skillet. Cook until the mussels and clams open. Remove the shellfish with a slotted spoon as they open and place in a large bowl. Cool to room temperature. Detach the meat from the shells and discard the shells. Place mussels and clams in a large salad bowl, cover, and keep refrigerated until ready to use.

3. Strain the liquid through a few layers of paper towels into a small bowl to remove any sandy deposits. Wipe out skillet and return strained liquid to the skillet. Put the skillet back on high heat and cook until only one or two tablespoons of concentrated, flavorful liquid are left in the pan. Place in a small bowl and cool to room temperature. Whisk the vinegar and remaining olive oil into the cooled liquid until it is well emulsified.

4. Add the garlic, chives, capers, onion, anchovies (if using), and diced tomatoes to the shellfish. Season with salt and several twists of pepper. Pour the dressing over the shellfish and mix well. Cover the bowl and leave on the counter to marinate for about one hour. Serve salad at room temperature with a few slices of grilled or toasted bread. *Makes 6 to 8 servings.*

Prepare ahead
Through step 3, several hours ahead. Cover and refrigerate.
Complete step 4, about one hour before serving.

TIP: Make sure to buy your shellfish from a reputable fishmonger. If any of the mussels or clams are open, tap them, and if they do not close, discard them.

Discard any shellfish that will not open during cooking. However, first give them a chance, since some need to cook a bit longer than others.

WHITE BEAN AND SMOKED SALMON SALAD

Chive is a member of the onion family. The bright green color of the long stems and the pronounced onion taste make chives a delightful addition to salads and soup. Cannellini beans are small white beans used extensively in Italian cooking.

2 pounds dried cannellini beans or white kidney beans

1 pound smoked salmon, cut into thin strips

2 medium red onions, very thinly sliced

3 to 4 tablespoons minced chives, or 2 tablespoons chopped fresh parsley

Salt and freshly ground pepper

$^1/_3$ to $^1/_2$ cup olive oil, preferably extra-virgin

$^1/_4$ cup red wine vinegar

1. Put the beans in a large bowl and cover with cold water. Soak the beans overnight. Drain and rinse thoroughly under cold running water.

2. Place the beans in a large saucepan and cover with cold water 2 inches above the level of the beans. Bring the water to a boil, then reduce the heat to low and simmer 40 to 50 minutes, or until the beans are tender. Drain beans, place in a large bowl, and cool. Set aside until ready to use.

3. Add salmon, onions, and chives to the beans, and season generously with salt and several twists of pepper. Dress with the oil and the vinegar, and mix gently to combine. Taste, adjust the seasoning, and serve. *Makes 8 to 10 servings.*

Prepare ahead
Through step 2, several hours or a day ahead. Cover and refrigerate.
Complete step 3, 10 to 15 minutes before serving.

◀ White Bean and Smoked Salmon Salad

SAVORY PIZZA WITH SWEET AND SOUR ONIONS

With a little imagination, this dish can be given several new identities. Sautéed mushrooms, strips of roasted peppers, or cooked spinach tossed in butter and parmesan can be substituted for the onions. Smoked ham or smoked turkey can be used instead of regular ham, and any good soft melting cheese can replace the mozzarella. Try several variations, and find the one you like best.

1 recipe Basic Pastry Dough (see page 75)	Salt
¼ cup olive oil	10 ounces thinly sliced ham
2 medium yellow onions, thinly sliced	10 ounces whole milk mozzarella, finely diced by hand or with a food processor
¼ cup sugar	1½ pounds firm ripe plum tomatoes, cut into ¼-inch round slices
¼ cup red wine vinegar	

1. Prepare the Basic Pastry Dough, substituting 1 teaspoon of salt for the sugar in the recipe. Shape into a ball and refrigerate for one hour.

2. Heat the oil in a large skillet over medium-high heat. Add the onions and cook, stirring, until they begin to color, 5 to 6 minutes. Add the sugar and vinegar, and season with salt. Raise the heat, and cook, stirring, until vinegar is evaporated, 1 to 2 minutes. Transfer onions to a strainer and put over a bowl to drain all liquids. Set aside until ready to use.

3. Preheat the oven to 375°F. Butter a pizza pan or 12 × 16-inch rectangular baking sheet.

4. On a lightly-floured surface, roll out the dough into a large rectangle that will just slightly overlap the baking sheet you are using. Place the dough on the baking sheet, pressing it gently to fit evenly. Fold the hanging dough to form a raised border, and pinch it with your fingertips to make a pattern. Prick the bottom of the dough with a fork in several places to prevent it from puffing up while baking.

5. Line the dough with the slices of ham and spread the onions evenly over the ham. Top the onions with the mozzarella and arrange the sliced tomatoes over the cheese. Season lightly with salt.

6. Bake until the crust has a nice, golden color, 20 to 25 minutes. Remove from oven. Leave pizza at room temperature a few minutes to allow the cheese to settle. Cut into squares and serve. *Makes 10 to 12 servings.*

Prepare ahead
Through step 5, one hour ahead. Keep pizza tightly wrapped in the refrigerator. Bake the pizza, step 6, about 30 minutes before serving time.

Cookery is not chemistry. It is an art. It requires instinct and taste rather than exact measurements.
—Marcel Boulstin

BRUSCHETTA WITH GRILLED TOMATOES AND PANCETTA

This kind of food is tasty, simple, and immensely appetizing. Even though this dish is particularly good in summertime when tomatoes are at their best, it can be prepared anytime when acceptable tomatoes are in the market. To improve the taste of winter tomatoes, season them generously and top them with a few sun-dried tomatoes. If you are using a large loaf of bread, serve only one slice per person. If you are using a long thin loaf of bread, such as a French baguette, serve 2 slices per person. (Keep in mind this is only an appetizer.) To serve the bruschetta warm, grill or broil the bread a few hours ahead, and reheat it in the oven just before topping it with the tomatoes and pancetta.

4 tablespoons extra-virgin olive oil

2 to 3 slices of pancetta or Canadian bacon, cut into small strips

8 slices crusty Italian bread

3 garlic cloves, peeled and halved

1 pound ripe juicy tomatoes, sliced into 1/4-inch thick rounds

Salt and freshly ground pepper

8 to 10 fresh basil leaves shredded, or 1 to 2 tablespoons freshly chopped parsley

1. Heat 1 to 2 tablespoons of the olive oil in a small skillet over medium heat. Add the pancetta and cook until it is golden brown and crisp, 1 to 2 minutes. With a slotted spoon, transfer pancetta to paper towels to drain. Place pancetta in a bowl and set aside until ready to use.

2. Preheat the broiler or heat the oven to 400°F. Put the bread on a baking sheet and toast under the broiler or in the oven, until the slices are golden on both sides. Rub one side of bread with garlic.

3. Put the bread slices on a serving platter and arrange the tomatoes over the bread. Season with salt and pepper, drizzle with the remaining olive oil, top with pancetta and basil, and serve. *Makes 8 servings.*

Prepare ahead
Through step 2, several hours ahead. Refrigerate pancetta.
Complete step 3, 15 to 20 minutes before serving.

LOVING DINNERS FOR FAMILY

Entrées

Baked Rigatoni with Bolognese Meat Sauce and Béchamel

Pasta with Uncooked Tomatoes and Fresh Herbs

Roasted Salmon with Salsa Verde and Tomato Condiment

Roasted Capon with Roasted Potatoes and
Ten Cloves of Garlic

Chicken and Red Bell Peppers with Cumin and Chili

Chicken Breasts with Curry Cream Sauce

Braised Rabbit with Gremolata and Soft Polenta

Veal Shanks with Jalapeño Peppers

Oven-Braised Veal Shanks with White Beans,
Smoked Bacon, and Rosemary

Skewers of Veal Bundles, Sausage, and Vegetables

Oven-Braised Beef Stew with Small Onions and Red Wine

Lamb Stew with Black Olives, Garlic, and Rosemary

Boneless Stuffed Lamb Roast

Roasted Pork Loin with Onion and Balsamic Vinegar

BAKED RIGATONI WITH BOLOGNESE MEAT SAUCE AND BÉCHAMEL

It is always a good idea to have a bit more sauce on hand to use if needed or to be refrigerated or frozen for later use.

For the Bolognese Meat Sauce

2 tablespoons unsalted butter

3 tablespoons olive oil

1 small onion, finely minced

1 small carrot, finely minced

1 small celery stalk, finely minced

1¹/₂ pounds ground veal

¹/₄ pound pancetta or Canadian bacon, chopped

1 cup dry white wine

3 cups canned imported Italian tomatoes with their juice, put through a food mill to remove the seeds

2 cups chicken broth

Salt and freshly ground pepper

(Makes about 4 cups)

For the Béchamel Sauce

2 cups milk

4 tablespoons unsalted butter

4 tablespoons all-purpose flour

Salt

(Makes about 1¹/₂ cups)

To Complete the Dish

1 tablespoon salt

1¹/₂ pounds rigatoni

1 cup freshly grated Parmigiano-Reggiano

2 to 3 tablespoons unsalted butter, cut into small pieces

1. *Prepare the meat sauce:* Heat the butter and oil in a large skillet over medium-high heat. When the butter foams, add the onion, carrot, and celery, and cook, stirring, until vegetables are lightly golden and soft, 4 to 5 minutes. Add the veal and pancetta, and cook, stirring, until the meat is lightly colored, 5 to 6 minutes. Raise the heat to high and add the wine. Cook until wine is almost all reduced, 3 to 4 minutes. Add the tomatoes and broth, and season with salt and pepper. Bring the sauce to a boil. Reduce the heat to low and cover the skillet with the lid slightly askew. Cook 1 to 1$^{1}/_{2}$ hours, or until the sauce has a medium-thick consistency. Stir a few times during cooking.

2. *Prepare the Béchamel sauce:* Heat the milk in a small saucepan over low heat. Melt the butter in a medium saucepan over medium-low heat. When the butter foams, add the flour and stir the mixture with a wooden spoon for 2 to 3 minutes without letting the flour turn brown. Add the milk to the butter mixture all at once and mix quickly and energetically to prevent lumps. Season with salt and cook, mixing constantly, until the sauce has a medium-thick consistency and is smooth and velvety, 3 to 5 minutes. (If the sauce is too thick, add a bit more milk.) Remove from heat, cover the pan, and refrigerate until ready to use.

3. Preheat the oven to 400°F. Generously butter a large deep baking dish.

4. Bring a large pot of water to a boil over high heat. Add the salt and the rigatoni. Cook, uncovered, until the pasta is tender, but firm to the bite. Drain the pasta and place in a large bowl. Add the meat sauce, 1 cup of béchamel sauce, and $^{1}/_{3}$ cup of the cheese. Mix everything thoroughly and place in the baking dish. Sprinkle remaining cheese over the pasta and dot generously with butter.

5. Bake 10 to 15 minutes, or until the cheese is melted and pasta has a nice golden color. Serve hot. *Makes 6 to 8 servings.*

Prepare ahead
Step 1, the meat sauce can be prepared a day ahead. Cover and refrigerate. Reheat gently over low heat, when ready to use.
Step 2, the Béchamel sauce can be prepared a few hours ahead.
Step 4, the pasta can be cooked and assembled with the sauces about one hour ahead.
Step 5, bake the pasta just before serving.

PASTA WITH UNCOOKED TOMATOES AND FRESH HERBS

A cool, fresh sauce, tossed with a perfectly cooked, hot pasta, makes a divine combination. Keep in mind that the sauce should not be combined too far ahead of time or the tomatoes will release too much of their juices. Keep all your prepared ingredients at room temperature and assemble the sauce at the last moment. Then, the only thing to do when guests arrive is boil the pasta, toss it with the sauce, and serve.

Of course this dish could also become a most beautiful pasta salad!

$1/3$ to $1/2$ **cup olive oil, preferably extra-virgin**

2 garlic cloves, minced

5 large ripe tomatoes, seeded and diced

6 to 7 long green onions, white part only, diced

1 cup loosely packed fresh shredded basil leaves

$1/3$ **cup loosely packed fresh oregano leaves, or 2 tablespoons chopped fresh flat Italian parsley**

$1/4$ **cup minced chives**

Salt and freshly ground pepper

2 pounds penne or shells

$1/2$ **pound mozzarella, cut into small cubes**

1. Mix the oil and garlic in a small bowl. In a large bowl, combine all the remaining ingredients except the pasta and the mozzarella. Add the oil/garlic mixture and season with salt and pepper. Set aside.

2. Bring a large pot of salted water to a boil over high heat. Add the pasta and cook until tender but still a bit firm.

3. Drain pasta thoroughly and combine with the tomatoes. Add the mozzarella and season with several additional twists of pepper. Mix well, taste, adjust the seasoning, and serve. *Makes 6 to 8 servings.*

Prepare ahead
Through step 1, one hour ahead.
Steps 2 and 3, just before serving.

◀ Pasta with Uncooked Tomatoes and Fresh Herbs

ROASTED SALMON WITH SALSA VERDE AND TOMATO CONDIMENT

This is one of the easiest of all dishes since the salmon is already cut into portions and the cooking time is extremely short. Keep in mind that properly cooked fish should be a bit translucent on the inside. The general rule for fish cookery is 10 minutes per inch of thickness. If your fillets are thicker than one inch, cook them a few minutes longer. The high temperature of the oven will give the salmon a crisp texture on the outside and moist tender flesh on the inside.

Salsa verde is a classic northern Italian sauce that is generally served as a condiment with boiled meats or fish.

The fresh tasting tomato condiment is a great accompaniment to roasted, grilled, or barbecued meat or fish.

For the Salsa Verde

1 slice white bread without the crust, broken into pieces

³/₄ to 1 cup olive oil

2 to 3 tablespoons red wine vinegar

¹/₄ cup capers, drained and rinsed

3 garlic cloves

4 cups loosely packed fresh parsley sprigs, preferably Italian flat leaf parsley

4 flat anchovy fillets

1 tablespoon Dijon mustard

1 large red bell pepper, halved, seeded and finely diced

Salt and freshly ground black pepper

(Makes 1¹/₄ cups)

For the Tomato Condiment

5 large firm ripe tomatoes, seeded and diced

2 small white celery stalks, diced

¹/₂ medium red onion, diced

1 tablespoon capers, drained and rinsed

¹/₄ cup small green pitted olives, quartered

1 to 2 tablespoons chopped fresh parsley, preferably Italian flat leaf parsley

¹/₃ to ¹/₂ cup olive oil, preferably extra-virgin

2 tablespoons red wine vinegar

Salt and freshly ground black pepper

(Makes 3¹/₂ cups)

For the Salmon

Olive oil

8 salmon fillets, 1-inch thick (7 to 8 ounces each)

Salt and freshly ground black pepper

1. *Prepare the salsa verde:* In a small bowl, combine the bread, oil, and vinegar, and mix well with your hands. Soak bread for 5 to 6 minutes. Put the contents of the bowl in a food processor fitted with the metal blade. Add the capers, garlic, parsley, anchovies, and mustard, and pulse the machine on and off until everything is chopped very fine but not puréed. Transfer sauce to a bowl. Add the diced red bell peppers, and season with salt and pepper. Mix well to combine. Cover bowl and refrigerate until ready to use. (The sauce should have a medium-thick but loose consistency. Add a bit more oil if necessary.)

2. *Prepare the tomato condiment:* In a medium bowl, combine all the ingredients for the condiment and mix well. Taste and adjust the seasoning. Cover the bowl and refrigerate until ready to use.

3. Preheat the oven to 500°F.

4. *Prepare the salmon:* Brush a large baking sheet with olive oil and arrange salmon fillets in a single layer. Brush salmon lightly with oil and season generously with salt and black pepper. Roast 10 to 12 minutes, or until golden on the outside but still a bit translucent on the inside. Serve with a few tablespoons of the two condiments on each side of the salmon. *Makes 8 servings.*

Prepare ahead
Through step 2, several hours or a day ahead.
Step 4, prepare salmon on a baking sheet half an hour ahead, and roast it at the last minute.

ROASTED CAPON WITH ROASTED POTATOES AND TEN CLOVES OF GARLIC

A capon is a neutered male chicken with a moist, tender, delicate flesh. Capons are generally larger and plumper than other chickens, and when properly cooked, they melt in the mouth. Capons generally average between eight and ten pounds. A nine-pound capon will yield 14 to 15 nice size pieces, since the large breasts can be cut into two or three pieces. If using chickens, you might want to buy two, since a 3¹/₂ pound chicken cuts into eight small pieces.

Paprika is a bright red powder made from a variety of peppers native to South America. The taste of paprika varies from mild to hot to sweet. Paprika is the national spice of Hungary.

1 capon, (8¹/₂ to 9 pounds), cut into 14 to 15 pieces

Salt and freshly ground pepper

2 tablespoons chopped fresh rosemary, or 1 tablespoon dried rosemary, crushed

2 tablespoons chopped fresh sage, or 1 tablespoon finely-crumbled dried sage

2 garlic cloves, minced

1 cup olive oil

1 tablespoon hot paprika powder

3 pounds potatoes, peeled, cut into 2-inch pieces, and covered with water

10 whole garlic cloves, peeled

2 tablespoons red wine vinegar

1. Rinse capon pieces thoroughly under cold running water and pat dry with paper towels. Put pieces in a large bowl and season generously with salt and several twists of pepper. Combine the rosemary, sage, minced garlic, and olive oil in a small bowl and add to capon. Sprinkle with the paprika and mix thoroughly to coat the capon pieces. Set aside for about one hour, turning the pieces in the marinade a few times.

2. Preheat the oven to 450°F. Heat a large roasting pan in the oven.

3. Drain potatoes and pat dry with paper towels. Add potatoes and whole garlic cloves to the bowl with the capon and mix well to coat. Put capon, potatoes, and all of the marinade into the hot roasting pan, and spread evenly in pan. (There should be a sizzling sound when the mixture hits the roasting pan.) Roast for 20 to 30 minutes, then reduce the heat

◀ Roasted Capon with Roasted Potatoes and Ten Cloves of Garlic

to 400°F and continue roasting for 45 minutes to one hour, or until the capon pieces are cooked through and the potatoes are golden brown. Baste with the pan juices and stir gently a few times.

4. Put the capon and all the potatoes and garlic on a large serving platter. Discard some of the fat from the pan and stir in the vinegar. Scrape the bottom of the pan with a wooden spoon. Spoon pan juices over capon and potatoes, and serve at once. *Makes 6 to 8 servings.*

Prepare ahead
Through step 1, one hour before roasting.
Step 2, preheat the oven and heat up the roasting pan at least 15 minutes before step 3.
Step 3, put capon in the oven about 1¹/₄ hours before you want to have dinner.
Complete step 4 just before serving.

TIP: Halfway through the cooking, you will probably find a large amount of liquid in the pan produced by the fat, and if frozen, by the watery juices of the bird. Simply spoon out as much of the liquid as you can and add a bit of additional olive oil.

At the end of the cooking, the garlic and potatoes will be soft and probably break into pieces. This is fine, for they will taste even better.

The capon can be kept in the marinade for several hours or overnight in the refrigerator. In that case, bring it completely to room temperature before roasting.

CHICKEN AND RED BELL PEPPERS WITH CUMIN AND CHILI

This delicious, easily-prepared chicken has a Middle Eastern flavor. Serve it over steamed or boiled rice, with couscous, grilled or soft creamy polenta (page 182), or simply by itself.
Cumin is the dried seed of an annual plant, with a distinctively pungent, hot taste. It is very popular in Middle Eastern, Mexican, and North African cooking.

$^1/_2$ **cup olive oil**

4 large chicken breasts (3$^1/_2$ to 4 pounds), skinned, boned, and cut into 1$^1/_2$-inch long strips

2 large onions, sliced into medium strips

4 large red bell peppers, halved, seeded, and cut into medium strips

1 cup dry white wine

5 to 6 cups canned plum tomatoes with their juice, put through a food mill to remove the seeds

2 tablespoons ground cumin

1 tablespoon chili powder

$^1/_2$ **to 1 teaspoon ground red pepper**

Salt

$^1/_3$ **cup chopped cilantro or flat leaf Italian parsley**

1. Heat the oil in a large skillet over medium-high heat. Add the chicken and cook until it is golden on all sides, 5 to 6 minutes. (Make sure not to crowd the skillet or chicken will not brown evenly. Brown chicken in a couple of batches if necessary.) With a slotted spoon, transfer chicken to a platter.

2. Discard half of the fat and add the onions and bell peppers to the skillet. Reduce heat to medium and cook, stirring, until onions and peppers are lightly golden, 5 to 6 minutes. Add the wine and cook until it is reduced by half, 3 to 4 minutes. Add the tomatoes, cumin, chili powder, and ground red pepper. Season with salt.

3. Return chicken to the skillet and reduce heat to low. Cover the skillet and simmer 15 to 20 minutes. Stir a few times during cooking. Add the chopped cilantro or parsley. Taste, adjust the seasoning, and serve hot. *Makes 8 servings.*

Prepare ahead
Through step 3, several hours or a day ahead. Cover and refrigerate.
If refrigerated, gently reheat it just before serving.

CHICKEN BREASTS WITH CURRY CREAM SAUCE

Curry powder is a blend of many aromatic spices. This beautiful dark orange powder has an intense aroma and flavor and is associated with East Indian cooking.

If the sauce is too thin at the end of cooking, transfer chicken to a large platter and keep it warm in a low oven. Raise the heat under the casserole and cook at a fast boil, stirring constantly, until sauce is a medium-thick consistency. Spoon over chicken and serve.

$1/2$ **cup olive oil**

8 large chicken breasts (7 to 8 pounds), boned and split

2 medium onions, thinly sliced

2 garlic cloves, minced

3 medium, firm ripe tomatoes, halved, seeded, and diced

$1^1/2$ **cups dry white wine**

Salt and freshly ground pepper

1 to $1^1/2$ cups heavy cream

Grated peel of 1 lemon

Juice of 2 lemons

$1^1/2$ **tablespoons curry powder**

1 to 2 tablespoons chopped fresh parsley

1. Heat the oil in large heavy casserole over medium-high heat. Add the chicken breasts, skin side down, and cook until golden on both sides, 5 to 6 minutes. (Do not crowd the casserole or the chicken will not brown evenly. Brown breasts in a few batches if necessary.) Transfer the chicken to a plate.

2. Discard half the fat in the casserole, reduce the heat to medium, and add the onion. Cook, stirring, until onion is lightly golden, 4 to 5 minutes. Add the garlic and the diced tomatoes. Stir a minute or two, then raise the heat to high and add the wine. Bring the wine to a boil and let it bubble for a few minutes until it is slightly reduced.

3. Return chicken to the casserole and season with salt and pepper. Cover, leaving the lid slightly askew, and reduce the heat to low. Simmer until the chicken is cooked all the way through, 15 to 20 minutes.

4. In a small bowl, combine the cream, lemon peel, lemon juice, and curry, and add to the chicken. Raise the heat to medium and bring the cream to a gentle boil. Cook, stirring, until sauce reduces and thickens a bit, 2 to 3 minutes. Stir in the parsley. Taste, adjust the seasoning, and serve at once. *Makes 8 servings.*

Prepare ahead
Through step 3, a few hours ahead. Cover and refrigerate.
Reheat the chicken gently and complete step 4 just before serving.

> *. . . some of us, considering cooking as an art, feel that a way of cooking can produce something that approaches an esthetic emotion. What more can one say?*
> —Alice B. Toklas

BRAISED RABBIT WITH GREMOLATA AND SOFT POLENTA

Gremolata is a mixture of herbs, garlic, anchovies, and grated lemon peel, which is added to the classic ossobuco alla Milanese. This delicious mixture imparts a subtle, very appetizing taste to the meat.

For the Rabbit

$^1/_2$ **cup olive oil**

2 cups all-purpose flour

3 large rabbits, $3^1/_2$ to 4 pounds each, cut into serving pieces, washed and dried on paper towels

Salt and pepper

3 medium carrots, diced

3 celery stalks, diced

1 medium onion, diced

$^1/_4$ pound sliced pancetta or Canadian bacon, finely diced

2 cups light red wine such as a pinot

2 cups chicken broth

2 cups canned plum tomatoes with their juice, put through a food mill to remove the seeds

For the Gremolata

3 garlic cloves, minced

2 to 3 tablespoons chopped parsley

3 to 4 flat anchovy fillets, chopped (optional)

Grated peel of 2 lemons

1. *Prepare the rabbit*: Heat oil in a large casserole over medium-high heat. Dredge the rabbit pieces lightly with flour and shake off the excess. Add pieces to the hot oil, making sure not to crowd them, and cook until they are golden on both sides, 6 to 7 minutes. (The rabbit can be browned in a few batches.) Season with salt and pepper. Transfer rabbit to a large platter.

2. Reduce the heat to medium and add the vegetables to the casserole. Cook, stirring, until vegetables begin to color, 4 to 5 minutes. Add pancetta. Cook until it is lightly golden, 4 to 5 minutes.

3. Return the rabbit to the casserole, raise the heat to high, and add the wine. Cook, stirring, 3 to 4 minutes, then add the broth and the tomatoes, and bring to a boil. Reduce the heat to medium low, and cover the casserole, leaving the lid slightly askew. Simmer about 1 hour or until rabbit is tender and sauce is of a medium-thick consistency. Transfer

◀ Braised Rabbit with Gremolata and Soft Polenta

rabbit to a large serving platter and keep warm in a low-heated oven while you finish the sauce.

4. *Prepare the gremolata:* Add garlic, parsley, anchovies, and lemon peel to sauce. Cook, stirring, for a few minutes. Taste and adjust the seasoning. Spoon sauce over rabbit and serve next to soft polenta. *Makes 8 servings.*

Prepare ahead

Through step 3, several hours or a day ahead. Cover and refrigerate.
Before serving, reheat rabbit gently over medium-low heat, and prepare the gremolata.

For the Polenta

9 cups cold water

2 tablespoons salt

2 cups coarsely ground cornmeal mixed with 1 cup finely ground cornmeal

1. Bring the water to a boil in a medium-size, heavy saucepan over high heat. Reduce the heat to medium, and add the salt. Start pouring handfuls of cornmeal slowly through your fingers, stirring constantly with a long wooden spoon or a large whisk to avoid lumps. When all the cornmeal has been incorporated, pour the polenta into a large stainless steel bowl and put the bowl over a large pan that contains 3 to 4 inches of simmering water. (Make sure that the water does not touch the bowl.) Cover the bowl with a lid or with foil and simmer approximately $1^1/2$ hours. Stir occasionally during cooking. Make sure that there is always enough simmering water in the pan. When done, the polenta will be thick and will come away cleanly from the side of the pot. *Makes 8 servings.*

TIP: If you need to hold polenta for a while, keep it tightly covered over barely simmering water. Stir it a bit before serving. For additional taste and smoothness, stir some butter and Parmigiano into the polenta during the last few minutes of cooking.

VEAL SHANKS WITH JALAPEÑO PEPPERS

This dish has a Southwest flavor given by the jalapeños, cilantro, and lime, which complement the delicate taste of veal quite well. Feel free to reduce the amount of jalapeños if the spiciness in the dish is too much for you.

Jalapeño peppers are widely used in Mexican and Southwestern cooking. This fiery pepper has a smooth thick flesh and a dark green color. Jalapeños can be kept tightly wrapped in the refrigerator for about a week.

8 large meaty veal shanks (5 to 6 pounds), cut 1½-inches thick

1 cup all-purpose flour

⅓ cup olive oil

2 medium red onions, thinly sliced

3 to 4 small jalapeños, seeded, white part removed, and minced

4 large tomatoes, halved, seeded, and diced

3 garlic cloves, minced

1 cup dry white wine

6 cups chicken broth

Salt

1 tablespoon chopped fresh oregano, or chopped fresh parsley

1 tablespoon chopped fresh cilantro

4 long green onions, white part only, thinly sliced

Juice of 1 lime

1. Dredge the veal shanks in flour and shake off any excess. Heat the oil in a large, heavy casserole over medium-high heat. Add the shanks and cook until golden on both sides, 6 to 7 minutes. Transfer shanks to a dish.

2. Reduce the heat to medium, and add the onions and jalapeños to the casserole. Cook, stirring, until onions are lightly golden, 5 to 6 minutes. Add tomatoes and garlic, and cook, stirring, 2 to 3 minutes. Raise the heat to high and add the wine. Cook and stir until wine is reduced by half, 3 to 4 minutes. Add chicken broth and bring to a boil.

3. Return shanks to casserole, season with salt, and reduce the heat to low. Cover casserole leaving the lid slightly askew. Simmer 1 to 1½ hours or until the meat is tender and begins to fall away from the bone. Stir and baste the meat a few times during cooking. Add a bit more broth if sauce reduces too much. Transfer the shanks to a large serving platter and keep warm in a low heated oven while you finish the sauce.

4. Add the oregano, cilantro, green onions, and lime juice to the casserole. Raise the heat to high and cook, stirring, until sauce has a medium-thick consistency, 2 to 3 minutes. Taste and adjust the seasoning, then spoon sauce over the meat and serve. *Makes 8 servings.*

Prepare ahead

Through step 3, several hours or a day ahead. Cover and refrigerate.

Before serving, reheat the veal gently over medium-low heat.

Transfer veal to a large platter and keep warm in a low-heated oven while you complete step 4.

All food is the gift of God and has something of the miraculous, the egg no less than the truffle.
—Sybille Bedford

OVEN-BRAISED VEAL SHANKS WITH WHITE BEANS, SMOKED BACON, AND ROSEMARY

Braised dishes such as this are perfect for a large crowd, since they can be completely prepared ahead of time and are generally better tasting if left to sit overnight.

$1/2$ **pound dried cannellini beans or white kidney beans, rinsed and sorted**

8 large meaty veal shanks (5 to 6 pounds), cut $1^1/2$ inches thick

1 cup all-purpose flour, spread on aluminum foil

$1/3$ **cup olive oil**

1 small yellow onion, minced

2 garlic cloves, minced

2 ounces thickly sliced smoked Canadian bacon, diced

4 to 5 large fresh sage leaves, chopped, or 1 teaspoon finely crumbled dried sage

2 tablespoons chopped fresh rosemary, or 1 teaspoon dried rosemary, crushed

$1/3$ **cup red wine vinegar**

3 cups chicken broth

3 cups canned plum tomatoes with their juice, put through a food mill to remove the seeds

Salt and freshly ground pepper

1 tablespoon chopped fresh parsley

1. Put the beans in a medium bowl and cover with cold water. Soak beans overnight. Drain and rinse beans thoroughly under cold running water.

2. Place beans in a medium saucepan, and cover with cold water 2 inches above the level of the beans. Bring the water to a boil, then reduce the heat to low and simmer 30 to 40 minutes, or until beans are tender but still a bit firm to the bite. Drain beans, place in a bowl, and set aside until ready to use.

3. Preheat the oven to 375°F. Dredge the veal shanks in flour and shake off any excess. Heat the oil in a large, heavy casserole over medium-high heat. Add the shanks and cook until golden on both sides, 6 to 7 minutes. Transfer the shanks to a dish.

4. Reduce the heat to medium, and add the onion to the casserole. Cook 2 to 3 minutes, stirring a few times. Add garlic, bacon, sage, and rosemary. Stir and cook until bacon is lightly golden, about 2 minutes.

5. Return the shanks to the casserole, raise the heat to high, and add the vinegar. Stir until vinegar is reduced by half. Stir in the broth and the tomatoes, season with salt and pepper, and bring liquid to a gentle boil. Cover the casserole, leaving the lid slightly askew, and place it in the oven. Bake 40 to 45 minutes.

6. Add the beans to the casserole and bake 20 to 30 minutes longer. Stir and baste the meat a few times during cooking. If the sauce thickens too much, add a bit more broth. At the end of cooking, the sauce should have a medium-thick consistency and the meat should begin to fall away from the bone. Stir in the fresh parsley, taste, adjust the seasoning, and serve. *Makes 8 servings.*

Prepare ahead
Through step 6, several hours or a day ahead. Cover and refrigerate.
Before serving, reheat the veal gently over medium-low heat.

SKEWERS OF VEAL BUNDLES, SAUSAGE, AND VEGETABLES

These skewers can be grilled, barbecued, or broiled. The cooking time will change slightly for each method. Fresh sage is an important component of this dish. If unavailable, do not use dry sage because it has a stronger, more pungent taste.

2 pounds mild Italian sausage, cut into 2-inch pieces

2 pounds veal scaloppine, pounded thin

$^1/_2$ pound prosciutto, sliced thin

$^1/_3$ cup freshly grated Parmigiano-Reggiano

6 ounces sliced pancetta or Canadian bacon, cut into small strips

24 fresh sage leaves

4 red bell peppers, halved, cored, seeded, and cut into 1-inch pieces

2 medium red onions cut into large chunks

$^1/_3$ to $^1/_2$ cup olive oil

Salt and freshly ground pepper

1. Bring a saucepan of water to a boil over medium-high heat. Add the sausage, turn off the heat, and let sausage sit in the hot water for 10 minutes. Drain sausage and place in a bowl of ice water to cool. Drain again and set aside until ready to use.

2. Place scaloppine on a work surface, and cover each one with a slice of prosciutto and 1 teaspoon of Parmigiano. (If prosciutto slices are too large, cut them in half.) Roll the veal into bundles and secure with one or two toothpicks. On metal skewers, alternately thread veal bundles, pancetta, sage, bell pepper, sausage, and onion. Set aside until ready to use.

3. Heat the oil in a large skillet over medium-high heat. Season meat lightly with salt and pepper, and place skewers in the hot skillet making sure to leave enough space between them. Cook until meat and vegetables are golden on all sides, 5 to 6 minutes. (The browning of the skewers should be done in several batches.) As they are done, transfer skewers to a large baking dish. Pour all of the oil and the pan juices in the skillet over the skewers.

4. Preheat the oven to 400°F. Place skewers in the oven, and bake until meat is cooked all the way through, 3 to 5 minutes. Baste once or twice with pan juices. Serve skewers on a bed of soft polenta (see page 182) or with steamed rice or mashed potatoes. *Makes 8 servings (16 skewers).*

Prepare ahead

Through step 2, several hours to a day ahead. Keep skewers tightly wrapped in the refrigerator.
Step 3 can be done about one hour ahead.
Complete step 4 just before serving.

. . . . How much good fortune has been the result of a good supper; at what moment of our existence are we happier than at the table? There hatred and animosity are lulled to sleep, and pleasure alone reigns.
—Anonymous

OVEN-BRAISED BEEF STEW WITH SMALL ONIONS AND RED WINE

When cooking stews or braised meats, always remember the following: After the initial browning done over high heat, the meat should simmer for a prolonged time to ensure moist, tender meat. The pot should always be covered but the lid should be left a bit askew. This allows the sauce to reduce slowly and to thicken. The meat should be basted or stirred several times during cooking, and the amount of liquid in the pot should be checked. If, at the end of cooking, you find that the sauce of the stew is too thin, transfer the meat to a platter and boil the sauce down to a thickness you like, then return the meat to the sauce. If the stew is left in the refrigerator overnight, bring it to room temperature and then reheat it gently over low heat.

For the Marinade

4 to 4^1/$_2$ pounds boneless beef chuck, cut into 2-inch pieces

4 to 5 cups red wine

2 onions, sliced

4 garlic cloves, crushed

^{1}/$_2$ cup red wine vinegar

For the Stew

2 pounds small white pearl onions, unpeeled

^{1}/$_3$ to ^{1}/$_2$ cup olive oil

6 ounces sliced pancetta or Canadian bacon, cut into small strips

2 tablespoons dried thyme

2 cups canned plum tomatoes with their juice, put through a food mill to remove the seeds

Salt and freshly ground pepper

1 to 2 tablespoons chopped fresh parsley

1. *Prepare the marinade:* Place the beef in a large bowl and add all the ingredients of the marinade. Mix well, cover the bowl, and marinate several hours or overnight.

2. *Prepare the stew:* Bring a medium saucepan of water to a boil over high heat and drop in the pearl onions. Cook 2 to 3 minutes. Drain and rinse under cold running water. Peel onions and set aside until ready to use.

3. Remove the meat from the marinade and pat dry with paper towels. Strain the marinade and reserve.

4. Preheat the oven to 375°F.

5. Heat the oil in a large, heavy, flame-proof casserole over medium-high heat. Add the beef in moderate batches and brown on all sides, 5 to 6 minutes. (Do not crowd the casserole or the beef will not brown evenly.) With a slotted spoon, transfer beef to a large platter.

6. Discard half of the fat and add the pancetta and thyme to the casserole. Cook, stirring, until pancetta begins to color, 1 to 2 minutes. Return beef to casserole and add the onions, 2 cups of the reserved wine marinade, and the tomatoes. Season with salt and several twists of pepper. Cover casserole, leaving the lid slightly askew, and place in the oven. Bake 1 to 1½ hours, or until the meat is tender. Stir and baste the meat a few times during cooking. Stir in the parsley and serve hot. *Makes 8 servings.*

Prepare ahead
Through step 6, several hours or a day ahead. Cover and refrigerate.
Reheat the stew gently over medium-low heat, just before serving.

Spread the table and quarrel will end.
—Anonymous Hebrew Proverb

LAMB STEW WITH BLACK OLIVES, GARLIC, AND ROSEMARY

This is an unpretentious but very flavorful dish that is perfect for a large gathering and takes well to reheating. Whenever possible, choose small black olives of intense flavor such as the imported Ligurian or Nicoise olives.

$^1/_3$ to $^1/_2$ cup olive oil

4 to $4^1/_2$ pounds boneless lamb shoulder, all fat removed and cut into 2-inch cubes

1 cup all-purpose flour

1 medium onion, finely minced

$^1/_2$ cup small pitted black olives, minced

1 tablespoon finely chopped fresh rosemary, or 1 tablespoon dried rosemary, crushed

2 garlic cloves, minced

A generous pinch of chili pepper flakes

Salt

1 cup full-bodied red wine

$^1/_3$ cup red wine vinegar

3 to 4 cups chicken broth

Grated peel of 1 lemon

Juice of 1 lemon

$^1/_2$ cup loosely packed fresh oregano leaves, or 2 tablespoons chopped fresh parsley

1. Heat the oil in a large, heavy, flame-proof casserole over medium-high heat. Place lamb in a large colander over a bowl and sprinkle with flour. Shake the colander to evenly distribute the flour. Add the lamb to the oil in small batches and brown on all sides, 5 to 6 minutes. (Make sure not to crowd the casserole or the lamb will not brown evenly.) With a slotted spoon, transfer lamb to a platter.

2. Discard half the fat and add onion to the casserole. Reduce the heat to medium and cook until onion is lightly golden, 5 to 6 minutes. Add olives, rosemary, garlic, and pepper flakes. Cook, stirring, about 1 minute.

3. Return lamb to casserole and season with salt. Toss well to mix lamb thoroughly with the onion mixture. Raise the heat to high and add the wine and vinegar. Cook, stirring, for 2 to 3 minutes, until wine and vinegar are slightly reduced. Add broth and bring to a boil. Cover casserole, leaving the lid slightly askew, and reduce the heat to low. Simmer 1 to $1^1/_2$ hours, or until the meat is tender. Baste and stir the lamb a few times during cooking. Add a bit more broth if sauce reduces too much.

4. Remove the lid and raise the heat to high. Add lemon peel, lemon juice, oregano, or parsley. Cook, stirring 1 to 2 minutes or until the sauce is a medium-thick consistency. Taste, adjust the seasoning, and serve hot. *Makes 8 to 10 servings.*

Prepare ahead

Through step 3, several hours or a day ahead. Cover and refrigerate.
Gently reheat stew and complete step 4 just before serving.

Cookery. . .the art that contains everything that is elegant and cautious
and without which all the other acts are useless. . . .
—M. Fagot

BONELESS STUFFED LAMB ROAST

Before the invention of the oven, meat was usually cooked on a spit or on a stove. Stove-cooked roasts were given a golden appetizing color over high heat and then finished cooking over low heat.

In this book, you will find that many roasts are browned on the stove ahead of time. The browning of the meat over high heat seals in juices, reduces the cooking time of the roast in the oven, and eliminates the last minute mess.

2 to 3 small sprigs fresh rosemary, chopped, or 1 tablespoon dried rosemary, crushed

4 garlic cloves, minced

$1/3$ to $1/2$ cup olive oil

1 leg of lamb, 8 to 9-pounds, boned, butterflied, and trimmed of all fat (will be approximately 5 pounds boneless)

Salt and freshly ground pepper

6 ounces prosciutto, thinly diced

1 to $1^1/2$ cups medium-bodied red wine, such as a pinot or chianti

1. In a small bowl, combine the rosemary, garlic, and 2 tablespoons of the olive oil. Place lamb on a flat surface and spread the rosemary mixture on the inner side of the lamb. Season with salt and pepper, and cover the meat with the prosciutto slices. Tightly roll the meat into a roast and tie securely with kitchen string. Rub the outside of the meat with a bit of olive oil and generously season with salt and pepper.

2. Preheat oven to 375°F. Heat remaining oil in a large, flame-proof casserole over medium-high heat. When the oil is very hot, add the lamb and brown on all sides, 7 to 8 minutes. (If the oil becomes too dark during the browning of the meat, discard it and add fresh oil.)

3. Place lamb in the middle of the preheated oven and roast 1 to $1^1/2$ hours for rare, or until it reads 145°F on a meat thermometer. For medium rare, cook to 150°F; for medium, cook to 160°F. Baste lamb with pan juices and with a bit of wine a few times during cooking.

4. Transfer the lamb to a cutting board and let it rest 15 to 20 minutes so that the meat will settle and the juices will evenly distribute inside the meat.

5. Discard about half of the fat and place the casserole on medium-high heat. Add remaining wine and bring to a boil. Cook and stir to pick up the bits and pieces attached to the bottom of the casserole. Cook until the wine is reduced by half, and the sauce has a thick consistency, 5 to 6 minutes.

6. Remove the string from the lamb. Slice the lamb and serve, topping it with a few tablespoons of pan juices. *Makes 8 servings.*

Prepare ahead
Through step 4, 20 minutes before serving.
Complete steps 5 and 6 just before serving.

ROASTED PORK LOIN WITH ONIONS AND BALSAMIC VINEGAR

Because of the fear of trichinosis, many people tend to overcook pork. Since pork is a dry meat, overcooking will result in a tough, stringy dish.

According to the National Pork Producers Council, harmful bacteria and trichinosis are eliminated when pork is cooked at an internal temperature of 137°F. When pork is cooked at 155°F, it is a perfectly cooked, barely pink, juicy, tender meat. Keep in mind that the meat will continue cooking as it rests and, within the 5-minute resting period, the internal temperature of the roast will probably be 160°F. If you don't have a meat thermometer, test the roast for doneness by piercing it with a thin knife or a skewer. If the juice comes out clear, the roast is done.

If you want to completely prepare the roast ahead of time, roast it to an internal temperature of 155°F, then turn off the oven. Cover the roast loosely with foil, and leave the oven door ajar. Let the roast settle in the oven for 15 to 20 minutes, then slice and serve it. At that point, the internal temperature of the roast should read 160°F to 165°F.

3 garlic cloves, minced

3 tablespoons chopped fresh rosemary, or 1 tablespoon dried rosemary, crushed

$^1/_3$ cup olive oil

4 to 5 fresh sage leaves, chopped (omit if not available)

4 pound boneless center cut, loin pork roast, securely tied

Salt and freshly ground pepper

1 cup dry white wine

3 large onions, thinly sliced

$^1/_3$ cup balsamic vinegar or red wine vinegar

1. Preheat the oven to 375°F.

2. Combine garlic, rosemary, and 1 tablespoon of the olive oil in a small bowl. With a thin knife, make several $^1/_2$-inch slits in the meat and fill them with the garlic mixture. Season roast well with salt and pepper.

3. Heat the remaining oil in a large heavy flame-proof casserole over medium-high heat. When the oil is very hot, add the pork and cook until it is golden on all sides, 7 to 8 minutes. Spoon off and discard about half of the fat in the casserole.

4. Raise the heat to high and add the wine. Cook and stir, turning the meat and scraping the bottom of the casserole with a wooden spoon, until the wine is almost all reduced, 5 to 6 minutes.

5. Place the casserole in the oven, and bake about 1 hour, or until the roast reads 130°F on a meat thermometer. Baste roast several times during cooking using pan juices or additional wine. Add the onions and half of the vinegar. Mix well, making sure onions are well coated with the oil and the pan juices. Bake 30 to 40 minutes longer or until roast reads 155°F on a meat thermometer. At this point, the onions should be soft, glazed, and perhaps a bit charred.

6. Transfer roast to a plate. Tilt the pan slightly, push the onions to one side, and spoon off some of the fat. Put the casserole on high heat, add remaining vinegar, and stir once or twice. Taste and adjust the seasoning. Return roast to casserole and cover with a lid. Let roast stand in the casserole off the heat for about one half hour before serving. At the time of serving, the roast temperature should read 160°F to 165°F.

7. Slice the roast and serve with some of the onions and a bit of the pan juices. *Makes 8 servings.*

Prepare ahead

Through step 6, a half hour before your guests arrive.
Complete step 7 just before serving.

LOVING DINNERS FOR FAMILY

Vegetables

White Beans with Rosemary, Sage,
and Sun-Dried Tomatoes

Gratin of Belgian Endive

Roasted Mushrooms and Potatoes with
Breadcrumb Topping

Sauté of Green Beans and Fresh Tomatoes

Baked Vegetables with Vinegar

WHITE BEANS WITH ROSEMARY, SAGE, AND SUN-DRIED TOMATOES

Select dried beans over canned beans, for they are more economical and have a taste and consistency that is far superior to canned beans.

3 pounds dried cannellini beans or white kidney beans, rinsed and sorted

$1/3$ to $1/2$ cup olive oil, preferably extra-virgin

2 tablespoons chopped fresh rosemary, or 1 teaspoon dried rosemary, crushed

1 tablespoon chopped fresh sage, or 1 teaspoon crumbled dried sage

2 to 3 garlic cloves, minced

3 tablespoons minced sun-dried tomatoes (packed in oil)

Salt and freshly ground pepper

1. Put the beans in a large bowl, and cover with cold water. Soak them overnight. Drain and rinse beans thoroughly under cold running water.

2. Place beans in a large saucepan and cover with cold water 2 inches above the level of the beans. Bring the water to a boil, then reduce the heat and simmer 40 to 50 minutes, or until the beans are tender. Drain beans, place in a large bowl, and cool. Cover bowl, and refrigerate until ready to use.

3. Heat the oil in a large skillet over medium heat. Add rosemary, sage, garlic, and sun-dried tomatoes. Cook and stir about 1 minute. Add beans, and season with salt and pepper. Cook just long enough to heat the beans through and to thoroughly coat them with the flavorful base of garlic, rosemary, sage, and sun-dried tomatoes. Serve warm. *Makes 8 to 10 servings.*

Prepare ahead
Through step 2, one or two days ahead.
Through step 3, a few hours ahead. Reheat the beans gently before serving.

GRATIN OF BELGIAN ENDIVE

The popularity of Belgian endive has grown considerably in the U.S. since it has become both more affordable and available. Belgian endive has a slightly bitter taste that becomes milder once it is cooked. It is delicious braised, baked, fried, or used raw in a salad.

8 large heads Belgian endive
(about 3 pounds)

1 cup chicken broth

4 ounces unsalted butter

Salt and white pepper

$^1/_3$ cup freshly grated Parmigiano-
Reggiano

1. Trim the root ends of the endive, and remove and discard any wilted leaves. Wash endive under cold running water.

2. Slice endive in half lengthwise, and place in a single layer, slightly overlapping, in a large flame-proof casserole. Add broth and 2 tablespoons of the butter. Cover and place on medium heat. Boil gently until broth is reduced by half and endive heads are tender but still a bit firm when pierced with a thin knife, 7 to 10 minutes depending on size.

3. Preheat the oven to 400°F. Season endive with salt and white pepper, sprinkle with cheese, and dot with butter. Bake in preheated oven until cheese is melted and endive has a golden color, 20 to 25 minutes. Serve warm. *Makes 8 servings.*

Prepare ahead
Through step 2, several hours ahead. Cover and refrigerate.
Complete step 3 about one hour ahead. Reheat them over gentle heat in the oven or on top of the stove, just before serving.

TIP: When selecting endive look for those that are compact, creamy white, and have no discoloration. Store endive tightly wrapped in plastic bags in the refrigerator.

ROASTED MUSHROOMS AND POTATOES WITH BREADCRUMB TOPPING

4 to 5 slices of bread, crust removed

Salt and freshly ground pepper

3 tablespoons chopped fresh parsley

$^1/_2$ cup olive oil

6 boiling potatoes (about 3 pounds), peeled and cut into $^1/_4$-inch round slices

$1^1/_2$ pounds white cultivated mushrooms, wiped clean and thinly sliced

1 garlic glove, minced

2 tablespoons unsalted butter, melted

$^1/_3$ cup freshly grated Parmigiano-Reggiano

1. Put bread in a food processor fitted with the metal blade and process into crumbs. (This should yield about 1 cup of bread crumbs. Add a few more slices of bread if necessary.) Place bread crumbs in a medium bowl, season with a pinch of salt and pepper, and toss with 2 tablespoons of the parsley and $^1/_4$ cup of olive oil (mixture should be moist). Set aside until ready to use.

2. Bring a large pot of water to a boil over medium-high heat. Add the sliced potatoes and cook, uncovered, until potatoes are tender but still a bit firm to the bite, 8 to 10 minutes. Drain and set aside until ready to use.

3. Heat the $^1/_4$ cup of the oil in a large skillet over high heat. Add mushrooms without crowding the skillet and cook, stirring, until mushrooms are lightly golden (if necessary, brown mushrooms in two batches). With a slotted spoon, transfer mushrooms to a bowl and pat gently with paper towels to remove excess oil. Stir in garlic and 1 tablespoon of the parsley, season lightly with salt and pepper, and mix well.

4. Preheat the oven to 400°F. Place potatoes in a large baking dish and season with salt. Add melted butter and cheese, and mix well. Spread potatoes to cover the bottom of the dish evenly. Top potatoes with the sautéed mushrooms and sprinkle the bread mixture over all.

5. Preheat the oven to 400°F. Bake 15 to 20 minutes, or until the bread crumbs are golden and vegetables are heated through. *Makes 8 to 10 servings.*

Prepare ahead

Through step 4, several hours ahead.
Complete step 5 just before serving.

SAUTÉ OF GREEN BEANS AND FRESH TOMATOES

2 pounds green beans, the smallest available

2 pounds ripe tomatoes

¹/₄ cup olive oil, preferably extra-virgin

2 garlic cloves, thinly sliced

2 anchovy fillets, chopped (optional)

Pinch of chili pepper flakes

Salt and pepper

1. Snap off both ends of the beans and wash under cold running water. Bring a large saucepan half full of salted water to a boil over medium-high heat. Add the beans and cook, uncovered, until tender but still firm to the bite, 2 to 4 minutes depending on size. Drain and immediately plunge them in a large bowl of ice water. This will stop the cooking but maintain the green color. When cool, drain the beans, and set aside.

2. Bring another medium saucepan half full of salted water to a boil over medium-high heat. Add the tomatoes and cook until the skins begin to split, about one minute. With a slotted spoon, transfer tomatoes to a bowl of ice water to cool. Peel and seed tomatoes and cut them into small strips. Place tomato strips in a strainer and place the strainer over a bowl to release the juice. Set aside until ready to use.

3. Heat the oil in a large skillet over medium heat. Add the garlic and the anchovies (if using). Stir for about one minute. Add the tomato strips and cook 2 to 3 minutes or until the juice of the tomatoes have thickened. Add beans and season with pepper flakes, salt and several generous twists of pepper. Cook just long enough for the beans to heat through, 1 to 2 minutes. Serve warm. *Makes 8 servings.*

Prepare ahead
Through step 2, several hours ahead.
Complete step 3, just before serving.

BAKED VEGETABLES WITH VINEGAR

This dish is an example of good, uncomplicated cooking, and an appreciation of simple straightforward food done the "old fashioned way." The "magic" ingredient added at the end of cooking is the vinegar, which turns the vegetables into a very appetizing treat.

2 pounds Japanese eggplant with skin on, cut into 2-inch pieces, or regular eggplant, the smallest available

2 medium onions, thickly sliced

4 red bell peppers (about 2 pounds), halved, cored, seeded, and cut into 2-inch strips

4 to 5 whole garlic cloves, peeled

Salt and freshly ground pepper

$1/4$ to $1/3$ cup olive oil, preferably extra-virgin

$1/4$ to $1/3$ cup red wine vinegar

1 to 2 tablespoons chopped flat leaf parsley or regular parsley

1. Preheat the oven to 400°F.

2. Put vegetables and whole garlic cloves in a large baking pan, season with salt and pepper, and toss with olive oil. Bake until vegetables are soft and golden in color, 40 to 50 minutes.

3. Remove vegetables from the oven, add the vinegar and the chopped parsley, and mix well. Serve warm or at room temperature. *Makes 8 to 10 servings.*

Prepare ahead
Through step 3, several hours ahead.
If the vegetables are to be served warm, reheat them briefly in the oven or on the stove.

TIP: If using regular eggplant, halve lengthwise and cut crosswise into $1/2$-inch slices.

LOVING DINNERS FOR FAMILY

Desserts

Mocha Ice Cream

Raspberry Tiramisù

Double Chocolate Trifle

Date, Raisin, and Plum Jam Tart

Apricot Tart

Apple Crumb Cake

Three Cheeses Cheesecake with Italian Wild Cherries

Butternut Squash Cheese Pie

Chocolate Almond Cookies

MOCHA ICE CREAM

For the Custard

6 cups milk

1 vanilla bean

12 large egg yolks

1¹/₄ cups sugar

For the Mocha

2 cups heavy cream

¹/₄ cup instant espresso or
regular coffee powder

¹/₂ pound semisweet chocolate,
cut into small pieces

1. *Prepare the custard:* Heat the milk and vanilla bean in a large saucepan over moderate heat. Remove from heat before milk boils.

2. In a large bowl or in the bowl of an electric mixer, beat the egg yolks and sugar until they are pale yellow and form soft ribbons, about 10 minutes. Add the milk to the eggs very slowly, a little at a time, beating after each addition. Transfer the mixture to the saucepan and place over medium-low heat. Beat constantly without letting the milk boil, cooking the custard for 5 to 6 minutes. (The custard is done when it coats the back of a spoon evenly.)

3. Discard the vanilla bean and strain the custard into a clean bowl. (The custard can be prepared up to this point a few days ahead and kept tightly covered in the refrigerator.)

4. *Prepare the mocha:* Combine the heavy cream with the espresso in a small saucepan. Heat the cream but do not boil it over medium heat, mixing with a wire whisk. Add the chocolate and mix until it is melted. Remove from heat, and chill in refrigerator.

5. Combine the custard with the mocha mixture. Place everything in the bowl of an ice cream maker and follow manufacturer's instructions. *Makes about 2 ¹/₂ quarts.*

Prepare ahead
Through step 5, several hours or a few days ahead. Freeze.
Soften ice cream in the refrigerator before serving.

RASPBERRY TIRAMISÙ

5 large egg yolks	2 tablespoons sugar
1 pound mascarpone cheese	Juice of 1 lemon
Grated peel of 1 lemon	$^1/_2$ cup brandy
3 large egg whites, beaten with $^1/_4$ cup sugar to a medium-stiff consistency	2 (1 pound each) store-bought pound cakes cut lengthwise into $^1/_4$-inch thick slices
3 pints raspberries	Raspberries to garnish

1. In a large bowl, or in the bowl of an electric mixer, beat the egg yolks until pale yellow. Add mascarpone and grated lemon peel, and beat until thick and smooth. Fold the beaten egg whites thoroughly into the mascarpone.

2. In a food processor fitted with the metal blade, combine raspberries, sugar, lemon juice and half of the brandy, and process until smooth. Put mixture through a sieve to eliminate the seeds, then pour into a medium saucepan. Cook over medium heat, stirring a few times, until raspberry mixture is reduced and has a medium-thick consistency, 5 to 6 minutes. Transfer to a bowl and cool. Reserve about $^1/_3$ cup of puréed raspberries to decorate the cake.

3. Cover the bottom of a 9 × 13-inch baking dish with a layer of pound cake slices. Brush cake with half the remaining brandy. Spread half of the mascarpone mixture evenly over the pound cake, then spread the raspberry purée over the mascarpone. Place another layer of pound cake over the raspberry purée, brush with remaining brandy and top with remaining mascarpone, spreading it to a smooth, even consistency. In a thin stream, spoon the reserved raspberry purée in a zig-zag pattern over the mascarpone to form a decoration. Cover the dish and refrigerate until ready to use. *Makes 8 servings.*

Prepare ahead
This is a dessert that must be prepared several hours or a day ahead to allow the ingredients to firm up.
Just before serving, decorate with some fresh raspberries.

DOUBLE CHOCOLATE TRIFLE

This is one of the most glorious desserts ever, especially if you are a chocolate lover. A large bowl that is filled to capacity with three layers of sinfully-rich white and dark chocolate mousse, intertwined with layers of rum-soaked pound cake and fresh tasting raspberry sauce, is pure decadence.

For the Dark Chocolate Mousse

1 pound semisweet chocolate, cut into small pieces

5 large eggs, beaten in a medium bowl

2 cups heavy cream, beaten to a medium-stiff consistency

For the Pound Cake and Raspberry Sauce

2 (1 pound each) store-bought pound cakes, cut into $1/4$-inch thick slices

$1/2$ cup dark rum

2 pints fresh raspberries, or 2 bags (12-14 ounces each) frozen raspberries

2 tablespoons sugar

Juice of 1 large lemon

For the White Chocolate Mousse

$1/2$ pound white chocolate, cut into very small pieces

3 tablespoons cold water

2 teaspoons Grand Marnier

$1^1/3$ cups heavy cream beaten to a medium-soft consistency

Fresh raspberries or chocolate shavings to decorate the trifle

1. Prepare dark chocolate mousse: Put the chocolate in a medium bowl or in the top part of a double boiler. Set it over 2 inches of simmering water and stir a few times until melted. Set aside to cool. Add eggs to cooled chocolate, a little at a time, beating at low speed with an electric hand beater or with a small wire whisk. (Do not overbeat or chocolate will become too stiff.) Thoroughly fold whipped cream into chocolate.

2. Arrange $1/2$ of the pound cake slices in the bottom of a deep glass bowl and brush with rum. Combine raspberries, sugar, and lemon juice in the bowl of a food processor fitted with the metal blade, and process until smooth. Put the mixture through a sieve to remove the seeds. Spread $1/3$ of the raspberry purée over the cake and spread half of the dark chocolate mousse over the raspberry purée. Place half the remaining pound cake slices over the chocolate mousse, brush with rum, and top with half the remaining raspberry purée. Set aside.

3. *Prepare white chocolate mousse:* (See note on page 66 before beginning this step.) Put the white chocolate, water, and Grand Marnier in a medium bowl or in the top part of a double boiler. Set it over 2 inches of very gently simmering water and stir constantly until chocolate has melted. Set aside to cool. Fold the whipped cream into the cooled chocolate a little at a time. Immediately spread mousse over the raspberry purée.

4. Place one last layer of pound cake slices over the white chocolate and brush with rum. Spread remaining raspberry purée over the cake and top with the remaining dark chocolate mousse. Cover the bowl and refrigerate overnight.

5. Just before serving, decorate with fresh raspberries or shavings of dark or white chocolate. *Makes 10 servings.*

Prepare ahead

Through step 4, one or two days ahead.
Complete step 5 just before serving.

DATE, RAISIN, AND PLUM JAM TART

1 recipe Basic Pastry Dough (see page 75)

³/₄ pound pitted dates, finely minced

1 cup dry white wine

Juice of 1 large lemon

¹/₂ cup dark raisins, softened in 1 cup water for 20 minutes

1 to 1¹/₂ cups plum jam

Butter for the tart pan

1 medium egg, lightly beaten in a small bowl

1. Prepare the Basic Pastry Dough. Shape into 2 balls, one a bit larger than the other, and refrigerate for one hour.

2. In a saucepan, combine dates, wine, and lemon juice. Bring liquid to a boil, then lower the heat and simmer for 6 to 7 minutes, until all liquid is evaporated and dates are tender and soft. Stir a few times during cooking. Transfer dates to a bowl and cool to room temperature. Drain raisins and pat dry with paper towels. Mix dates thoroughly with raisins and jam. Set aside until ready to use.

3. Preheat the oven to 375°F. Butter a 10-inch tart pan that has a removable bottom.

4. On a lightly-floured surface, roll out the larger ball of dough to a 12-inch circle. Place the dough in the prepared tart pan and press gently to fit evenly in the pan. Trim edges of dough by pressing the rolling pin over top of pan. Press the dough gently but firmly up the sides of the pan going just a bit over the edges. Press the tines of a fork over the rim of the dough to form a pattern and prick the bottom of the shell in several places with the fork. Evenly spread the date mixture into the pastry shell.

5. Roll out remaining dough into a rectangle. Using a scalloped pastry cutter or a sharp knife, cut dough into 11-inch strips, ¹/₂-inch wide. Lay strips across the tart to make a lattice, pressing and pinching the strips onto the rim of the dough. Brush dough with the beaten egg.

6. Bake 30 to 40 minutes, or until the crust has a golden color. Cool tart completely before serving. *Makes 8 to 10 servings.*

Prepare ahead
Through step 6, several hours or a day ahead.

APRICOT TART

Mixed dried fruit simmered with wine and lemon juice and combined with walnuts and jam becomes the delectable base of this apricot tart. If the apricots you choose for the filling are soft and ripe, skip step 4 in the recipe, and simply place the uncooked apricots on the fruit mixture and continue as instructed.

In winter, substitute Bosc pears for the apricots. Peel pears and poach in red wine or marsala until cooked half way through. Slice pears in halves lengthwise, place on the fruit mixture, and continue as instructed.

$^1/_2$ **recipe of Basic Pastry Dough (see page 75)**

$^1/_2$ **pound dried fruit (apricots, pears, prunes, etc.), minced**

1 cup dry white wine

Juice of 1 lemon

$^1/_2$ **cup finely minced walnuts**

$^1/_2$ **cup apricot jam**

2 tablespoons honey

Butter for the tart pan

5 ripe, but firm apricots (about $^3/_4$ pound), halved and pitted

$^1/_3$ **cup sugar**

1 egg lightly beaten in a small bowl

$^1/_2$ **cup apricot jam**

3 to 4 tablespoons brandy, Grand Marnier, or rum

1. Prepare the Basic Pastry Dough. Shape into a ball and refrigerate for one hour.

2. Prepare the filling: In a small saucepan, combine the minced fruit, wine, and lemon juice. Bring the liquid to a boil, then lower the heat and cover the pan. Simmer fruit until all the liquid in the pan is evaporated and fruit begins to soften, 5 to 6 minutes. Stir a few times during cooking. Transfer fruit to a bowl and cool to room temperature. Mix the walnuts, jam, and honey into the fruit thoroughly, and set aside until ready to use.

3. Preheat the oven to 375°F. Butter a 10-inch tart pan that has a removable bottom.

4. Dip both sides of the apricots in sugar, place on a baking sheet cut side down, and bake until they begin to soften, 7 to 8 minutes. Set aside until ready to use.

5. On a lightly-floured surface, roll out the dough to a 12-inch circle. Place the dough into the prepared tart pan and press gently and evenly into the pan. If necessary, trim edges of dough with scissors, leaving some dough hanging over the rim. Fold the hanging dough to form a border and pinch it with your fingers to seal and to make a pattern. Prick bottom of shell in several places with a fork. Spread the fruit mixture into the pastry shell. Arrange fresh apricots cut sides down over the filling, and brush dough with beaten egg. Bake until crust is golden brown, 20 to 25 minutes. Cool tart to room temperature.

6. *Prepare the glaze:* In a small skillet, combine jam and brandy. Cook, stirring, for a few minutes. Brush apricots with glaze and refrigerate until ready to serve. *Makes 8 to 10 servings.*

Prepare ahead
Through step 6, several hours ahead. Serve tart just barely chilled.

. . . happy go lucky cooks who tell you, not without pride, 'of course I never follow a recipe, I just improvise as I go along. A little bit of this, a spoonful of that . . . it's much more fun really.' Well, it may be more fun for the cook, but it is seldom so diverting for the people who have to eat his products.
—Elizabeth David

APPLE CRUMB CAKE

This cake has a crumbly consistency with a filling that can be changed to suit the mood of the cook. Use pears instead of apples, jam instead of the honey, and dried figs or apricots instead of dates. One ingredient that should not be tampered with is the amount of butter. If you use less butter, the cake falls apart. It is important to cool and refrigerate the cake for a few hours before serving to allow it to firm up.

3 medium golden delicious apples, peeled, cored, and diced

$1/3$ cup golden raisins, soaked in lukewarm water for 20 minutes and drained

4 ounces dates or dried figs, finely minced

$1/3$ to $1/2$ cup honey

Butter for the tart pan

6 ounces hazelnuts

2 cups all-purpose flour

$1/2$ cup sugar

Grated peel of 1 lemon

8 ounces (2 sticks) unsalted butter, melted

1. In a medium bowl, combine apples, raisins, dates, and honey, and mix well. Set aside.

2. Preheat the oven to 350°F. Butter a 10-inch tart pan that has a removable bottom.

3. Place the hazelnuts in a single layer in a shallow ungreased baking pan, and bake until lightly golden, 3 to 4 minutes. Wrap hazelnuts in a large kitchen towel and rub off as much skin as possible. Chop the hazelnuts into very fine pieces in a food processor, pulsing the machine on and off. (Do not process into powder.) Place hazelnuts in a large bowl and combine with flour, sugar, lemon peel, and melted butter. Mix well with a wooden spoon, then rub mixture lightly with the palms of your hands to make small crumbs. Put half of the crumbs in the tart pan, lightly pressing them to the bottom of the pan.

4. Spread the apple mixture evenly over the crumbs and scatter remaining crumbs over apples. Bake until apples are tender and the top of cake is golden brown, 25 to 30 minutes. Cool cake on wire rack then refrigerate until serving time. Serve cake slightly chilled. *Makes 8 to 10 servings.*

Prepare ahead
Through step 4, several hours or a few days ahead. Leave cake at room temperature for about $1/2$ hour before serving.

THREE CHEESES CHEESECAKE WITH ITALIAN WILD CHERRIES

"Amarena Fabbri" are Italian wild black cherries preserved in heavy syrup. Amarene have a bittersweet taste which is most agreeable when paired with soft cheeses such as mascarpone. Because of the large amount of moisture in the cheeses and the cherries, this cake should be kept refrigerated until the time of serving. As with all cakes that have beaten egg whites, this cake will deflate and shrink a bit after baking.

1/2 recipe of Basic pastry Dough (see page 75)	**Grated peel of 2 lemons**
Butter for the cake pan	**4 large egg yolks**
1 1/2 pounds ricotta	**3 large egg whites, beaten to a stiff consistency**
3/4 pound mascarpone cheese	**8 ounces Amarene Fabbri cherries, drained of their juices and finely diced**
3/4 pound cream cheese	
3/4 cup sugar	**1 tablespoon all-purpose flour**

1. Prepare the Basic Pastry Dough, shape into a ball and refrigerate one hour. Butter a 9-inch springform cake pan.

2. On a lightly-floured surface, roll out the pastry dough and place in the buttered cake pan, leaving about 1 inch of dough hanging over the rim. Press gently to fit dough evenly into the pan. Fold the hanging dough to form a border, and pinch it with your fingertips to make a pattern. Refrigerate until ready to use.

3. Preheat the oven to 375°F. In a food processor, combine the cheeses and sugar, and process until smooth. Add lemon peel and egg yolks and process to incorporate. Transfer mixture to a large bowl and fold in the beaten egg whites.

4. In a small bowl, mix cherries with flour and spread on the bottom of the pastry shell. Add cheese mixture and shake the pan lightly to distribute the filling evenly. Bake for 15 minutes, then lower the heat to 325°F and bake until cake is golden brown or until a thin skewer inserted in the center comes out clean, 1 to 1 1/4 hours. Cool 30 minutes, then refrigerate cake for a few hours, or longer, before serving. *Makes 8 to 10 servings.*

Prepare ahead
Through step 4, several hours ahead or overnight.

BUTTERNUT SQUASH CHEESE PIE

Amaretti di Saronno are imported Italian almond cookies. These crisp cookies are often used as a component of many desserts and as stuffing for baked fruit or unusual pasta dishes. To crush the amaretti, place them between two sheets of plastic wrap and push a rolling pin back and forth, or pound them with a large knife or a cleaver.

For the Filling

2 medium butternut squash (about 3 cups cooked squash pulp)

8 ounces cream cheese

2 tablespoons heavy cream

1 cup sugar

6 pairs imported Amaretti di Saronno cookies, or 6 almond macaroons, crushed into small crumbs

1 cup freshly grated Parmigiano-Reggiano

4 large eggs, lightly beaten in a bowl

For the Pie Crust

4 ounces (1 stick) unsalted butter

1 1/2 cups graham cracker crumbs

8 pairs imported Amaretti di Saronno cookies, or almond macaroons, crushed into small crumbs

1. Prepare the filling: Preheat the oven to 400°F. Cut the squash in halves lengthwise and remove the seeds. Wrap squash in aluminum foil and bake until tender, 1 to 1 1/2 hours. When the squash is cool enough to handle, scoop out the pulp, and place it in a strainer over a large bowl. Mash the squash with a spoon, pressing it against the side of the strainer. Leave the squash in the strainer for about a half hour to drain.

2. Put the cream cheese, cream, and sugar in the bowl of a food processor, and pulse the machine on and off until the cheese is soft and creamy. Add the squash, cookie crumbs, and Parmigiano. Pulse the food processor on and off again, just long enough to blend the ingredients. (Do not process too long or the squash will become soupy.) Place mixture in a large bowl and thoroughly fold in the eggs. Cover and refrigerate a few hours.

3. Prepare the crust: Preheat the oven to 400°F. Melt the butter in a small skillet over medium-low heat and cool it slightly. Place butter in a bowl and combine it with the graham cracker crumbs and the crushed amaretti. Press some of this mixture firmly against the sides and bottom of a 10-inch springform cake pan. Carefully pour the butternut mixture into the center of the pan. Bake 15 minutes, then lower the heat to 350°F, and bake

30 to 40 minutes more. Keep your eyes on the pie. If the top becomes too dark, lower the heat to 300°F and bake it a bit longer. The pie is done when the top is golden brown and a thin knife inserted in the center of the pie comes out clean. Cool 30 minutes and refrigerate pie, a few hours or longer, to firm it up before serving. *Makes 8 to 10 servings.*

Prepare ahead
Through step 3, several hours or a day ahead. Serve slightly chilled.

Everything I eat has been proved by some doctor or another to be
a deadly poison, and everything I don't eat has been proved
to be indispensable for life . . . but I go marching on.
—George Bernard Shaw

CHOCOLATE ALMOND COOKIES

1^1/$_4$ **pounds blanched almonds**

^{1}/$_4$ **pound semisweet chocolate, finely chopped by hand or with a food processor**

^{3}/$_4$ **cup sugar**

2 cups all-purpose flour

1 teaspoon dry yeast

^{1}/$_2$ **teaspoon salt**

5 large eggs, lightly beaten in a small bowl

Butter for the cookie sheet

1 large egg, lightly beaten with 1 teaspoon water in a small bowl

1. Preheat the oven to 375°F. Place the almonds on a cookie sheet and bake until they are lightly golden, 6 to 7 minutes. Put the almonds in a food processor and pulse on and off until they are broken into very small pieces. (Do not process almonds into powder.)

2. In a large bowl, combine almonds, chocolate, sugar, flour, yeast, and salt. Mix well to combine. Add the eggs and mix with a wooden spoon or your hands to form into a soft paste. Put the mixture on a flat surface and work into a ball. Sprinkle the dough with flour if it sticks heavily to your hands. (Keep in mind, however, that the dough should be just a bit sticky.)

3. Butter and flour a cookie sheet. Divide the dough into 3 or 4 pieces. Lightly flour your hands and shape each piece of dough into a roll about 2 inches in diameter. Place rolls on the cookie sheet and brush them lightly with the beaten egg. Bake 20 to 25 minutes, or until they have a nice golden color.

4. Remove from the oven. As soon as the rolls are cool enough to handle, cut them diagonally into 3-inch long and ^{1}/$_2$-inch wide cookies. Turn the oven off, place the cookies back on the cookie sheet, and put them back in the oven for 15 to 20 minutes more. *Makes 25 to 30 cookies.*

Prepare ahead
Through step 4, several hours or several weeks ahead.
Cool cookies completely, then store in an air-tight container. They will keep well for several weeks.

HARMONY OF WINE AND FOOD

by René Chazottes

We could discuss and debate the merits and qualities of wine forever. These few words are not, therefore, meant to be a critique, but rather a simple guide to the harmony between wine and food.

A dinner is like an opera. The opera usually begins with an overture to set the theme and mood, followed by various acts, and ending with a finale and curtain call.

As with the opera, wines are generally served following one another in ascending order of their various characteristics. The score is simple. We always serve wines from the driest to the sweetest, from the lightest to the most powerful, from the oldest to the youngest.

It is important that we do not forget any of the progressive acts of the opera as the story is revealed; the same holds true with wine. A wine should never overpower the one that preceded it, causing us to forget it, nor should its qualities be lost because we followed it by a more powerful one, which has all but obliterated its subtleties.

L'apéritif is the opening act, the overture of a meal. This should create a mood of congeniality and pleasure, setting the scene for what is to come.

The best apéritif is a light, dry wine. Hard liquor can dull the palate. Ideally, a very good champagne or sparkling wine that is airy, neither heavy nor sweet, with a delicate and romantic effervescence, would be the apéritif of choice.

As with music, each instrument conveys a texture all its own; low and dark like a cello, high and light like a flute. Neither is better than the other, but when blended, both make beautiful music that neither could accomplish alone. So, too, with food and wine. Some wines are darker, more powerful; some lighter, more delicate. So like a composer, the chef strives to match wines and foods to the perfect balance and harmony. For example, with fowl and lighter meats, we lean toward brighter, less heavy wines than we would with a red meat dish. So it is with desserts and cheeses.

The feast is a pleasure we look forward to, and like going to the opera, not something we do every day. It is a special occasion.

Too much wine can bring on drowsiness, and as with somnolence at an opera, it would make for a sad conclusion to an evening. We know the opera and the dinner have both achieved their purpose when we leave either one eager for the next time!

René Chazottes is one of America's reigning Grand Sommeliers. He represented the United States in the 1990 Third Annual International Competition in Paris, where he finished first in the Harmony of Food and Wine competition. He currently serves as the Director of Wine for the Pacific Club in Newport Beach, California.

Some Loving Tips for the Chef

- Don't be intimidated by food preparation. Remember, it's just food.
- Don't be concerned that your guests may be better cooks than you. Dinner parties are not competitions.
- Relax and have fun while preparing your meals. A refreshing drink and music of your choice can work wonders.
- Try new recipes before you serve them to company. You'll feel more secure and confident if you do.
- When preparing a recipe, measure all ingredients and do all the preparation before actually beginning.
- Remember that a recipe is merely a guide. After you have tried it, feel free to give it your own touches. It is not etched in stone. (This is not true with baking.)
- Prepare a serving menu, checking off each item as you go. This prevents common mistakes such as leaving the rolls in the oven or the salad in the refrigerator.
- Purchase fresh ingredients whenever possible. It makes a big difference in appearance and taste. Attempting to save a few cents at the expense of quality is false economy.
- Add distinctive touches of beauty to your table and home wherever you can—fresh flowers, candles, interesting china—anything your creative mind and imagination can dream of. Ambiance ties all the other components together.
- Have a seating plan in mind. Putting the right people together can be vital to a successful evening.
- Planning more than an hour for hors d'oeuvres and aperitifs can be risky. You don't want your guests to fill up on appetizers or end up staggering to your table.
- Since no more than 5 to 10 minutes of final preparation is required for any recipe in this book, be certain to sit down with your guests and have fun. You deserve it. Anyone will wait five minutes for the next delectable course.
- Good dinner parties don't just happen. They are orchestrated with the same care that a maestro uses to prepare for a concert. That's the thrill of it. The evening is yours to program and conduct.
- Enjoy!

SOME LOVING TIPS FOR BEVERAGE SELECTION AND ENJOYMENT

- If you plan to serve alcoholic beverages, always have a choice of soft drinks available for those who do not take alcohol. Don't make a fuss about this, just give the guest something else. Nonalcoholic wines and sparkling drinks can be an interesting substitute.

- Don't be intimidated by wine. After all, it's simply crushed grapes and not worth fermenting over. Your wine merchant will be pleased to help you select the wine best suited to your meal.

- The general rule is white wine with white meats (fish, fowl, pork), and red wine with red meats. But there are several possible variations to this. Search for the wines you enjoy and which will enhance the food you are presenting. Experimentation is part of the joy of wine.

- It has always been believed that the elixir of love is champagne, and like love, it can be enjoyed at any time of the day or night. Like love, too, it blends with and enhances everything.

- Wine prices vary. The highest price does not guarantee the best wine. Shop for bargains. You will be surprised at how inexpensively you can find a good wine. "End of Bin" sales are always a good place to look.

- You may want to serve more than one wine with your dinner—a white wine with your crêpe cannelloni and a red wine with your pot roast.

- You can count on five glasses of wine from a regular 750 ml bottle.

- Always have an extra bottle of each wine you serve—just in case.

- Dessert wines are a lot of fun and can enhance your dessert course and post-dinner merriment.

- You are under no obligation to serve a wine that a guest may have brought as a house gift on the evening of your dinner. A heart felt "thank you" is enough.

- You don't have to be a connoisseur of wines to appreciate them, buy them, or serve them. But wine is exciting and fun, and the more you know about it, the more enjoyment you will have.

INDEX

EPILOGUE

There is an eloquent tale about the difference between Heaven and Hell. It is said that in both places, the occupants are presented with opulent tables laden with exotic foods and given four-foot long utensils with which to eat. In Hell, people are miserable and starving because they cannot imagine how to get food to their mouths with such long forks. In Heaven, the people are joyful and well fed. They use the same forks to feed each other.